I know from experience that raising kids is harder than raising the dead. I had to do both to my youngest son. He was dead for over four hours, in a morgue, with a toe tag on, and praise the Lord, he came back to life.

Duane and Sue Sheriff have raised four children who are all serving the Lord and raising their families in the love of the Lord. That is a modern-day miracle, and it hasn't happened by chance. In this book, Duane will share with you the truths that have worked for him, and God is no respecter of persons. He will do the same for you as you take hold of these biblical principles and apply them to yourselves and your children.

Andrew Wommack
President and Founder of
Andrew Wommack Ministries and
Charis Bible College

Raising GODLY WARRIORS

Harrison House Books by Duane Sheriff

Identity Theft: Satan's Greatest Crime Against Humanity

Erasing Offense: Defeating the Enemy's Scheme to Destroy Your Relationships

Better Together: How to Build a Marriage That Lasts

Divine Guidance: Hearing and Responding to the Voice of God

Rhythms of Grace: Experiencing Freedom from Fear, Worry, and Stress

Counterculture: Answering a Woke Culture with Love, Light, and Life

Our Union with Christ (Audible Audiobook)

Raising GODLY WARRIORS

BUILDING STRONG
FAMILIES IN
TODAY'S CULTURE

DUANE SHERIFF

© Copyright 2025– Duane Sheriff

Printed in the United States of America. All rights reserved. No portion of this book may be reproduced, stored in a retrieval system, or transmitted in any form or by any means—electronic, mechanical, photocopy, recording, scanning, or other—except for brief quotations in critical reviews or articles, without the prior written permission of the publisher.

Unless otherwise identified, Scripture quotations are taken from the New King James Version. Copyright © 1982 by Thomas Nelson, Inc. Used by permission. All rights reserved.

Scripture quotations marked KJV are taken from the King James Version.

Scripture quotations marked NIV are taken from the HOLY BIBLE, NEW INTERNATIONAL VERSION®, Copyright © 1973, 1978, 1984, 2011 International Bible Society. Used by permission of Zondervan. All rights reserved.

Scripture quotations marked NLT are taken from the Holy Bible, New Living Translation, copyright 1996, 2004, 2015. Used by permission of Tyndale House Publishers, Wheaton, Illinois 60189. All rights reserved.

Scripture quotations marked AMPC are taken from the Amplified® Bible, Classic Edition, Copyright © 1954, 1958, 1962, 1964, 1965, 1987 by The Lockman Foundation. All rights reserved. Used by permission.

Scripture quotations marked AMP are taken from the Amplified® Bible, Copyright © 2015 by The Lockman Foundation, La Habra, CA 90631. All rights reserved. Used by permission.

Scripture quotations marked MSG are taken from The Message. Copyright © 1993, 1994, 1995, 1996, 2000, 2001, 2002. Used by permission of NavPress Publishing Group. Used by permission. All rights reserved.

All emphasis within Scripture quotations is the author's own.

Published by Harrison House Publishers
Shippensburg, PA 17257

ISBN 13 TP: 978-1-6675-1114-6
ISBN 13 eBook: 978-1-6675-1115-3
ISBN 13 Hardcover: 978-1-6675-1117-7
ISBN 13 Large Print: 978-1-6675-1118-4

For Worldwide Distribution, Printed in the U.S.A.
1 2 3 4 5 6 7 8 / 29 28 27 26 25

Contents

Introduction		1
1	Parents as Watchmen	4
2	A Warrior's Arrows	8
3	Godly Seed	17
4	Rules	23
5	Restraints	34
6	Relationship	42
7	Good Communication	47
8	A Legacy of Faith	56

Training — 65

9	Every Child's Greatest Need	67
10	Rod of Correction	77
11	Provoke Not to Wrath	86
12	Blessing Our Children	92

Teaching — 99

13	Preparation Time	101
14	Building Healthy Esteem	110

15 The Power of Identity	122
16 Recreational Dating	127
17 Foundations by Adulthood	138
Transitioning	149
18 Different Kinds of Love	151
19 Sexual Purity	161
20 The Marriage Altar	170
21 A Biblical View on Sex	177
22 Preparing for Marriage	186
Conclusion	195
About the Author	197

Introduction

Like arrows in the hand of a warrior, so are the children of one's youth.

—*Psalm 127:4*

The biblical illustration of children as arrows is a beautiful and apt description of healthy parent-child relationships. Like a master craftsman builds and shapes an arrow for battle, so God gives children into our care to prepare them for their future. But notice children are *"arrows in the hand of a warrior"* (Psalm 127:4). Parenthood is a fight. Whether or not you recall the application you completed before becoming a mom or dad, parenting is not for the slothful or faint of heart.

Wimps need not apply!

If there was ever a time to be sober and vigilant in the parenting of our children, it is today. Everything in our culture wars against the family; it wars against parents. The lions of culture have arrayed themselves around our families as secular humanism, sexual perversion, identity confusion, digital addiction, drugs, and alcohol, to name only a few. These lions wait, eager to pounce on any lamb they find. Our job, as warriors, is to defend those lambs. We must take our role as parents seriously to resist these lions, standing steadfast in faith, and engage in our children's lives so that we don't lose an entire generation.

It only takes one generation of neglect to forget the ways of the Lord. Look at Israel. After Joshua and his generation—the generation who experienced God's care in the wilderness and saw His works as they entered the Promised Land—died, the Israelites did evil in the eyes of the Lord (Judges 2:10-11). They *"...served the Baals; and they forsook the Lord God of their fathers, who had brought them out of the land of Egypt..."* (Judges 2:11-12). And the people felt the consequences of that sin. Nations rose up against them to plunder them. They lost land; they lost lives and livelihoods (Judges 2:12-15). All because of one generation. One generation *"who did not know the Lord"* (Judges 2:10).

As parents, we must teach our children the ways of God, or, like Israel, they will perish. Our God is a generational God. He is the God of Abraham, Isaac, and Jacob. He thinks and works generationally. Yet, too often, we do not. We disengage from our role and allow our families to drift on the sea of life. But as an arrow is designed to accurately hit a specific target, parents are assigned to protect, prepare, and propel children into their futures despite the fallen world in which we live.

Our children were made to prosper. And we, as parents, were designed to succeed in our calling. But that success doesn't happen by accident. It requires partnership with the One who gave our children to us. Psalm 127:3 says, *"Behold, children are a heritage from the Lord, the fruit of the womb is a reward."* Heritage here simply means gift. Our children are gifts from God. They did not come from us; they came *through* us.

God entrusts children to us and partners with us as we raise them in the nurture of the Lord (Ephesians 6:4). Psalm 127:5 says, *"Happy is the man who has his quiver full of them."* Yet many quiver with just one. They wonder what sin they committed to be punished with such a strong-willed, misbehaving child. But that is not what parenting is supposed to feel like. God wants our family life to be a mutual blessing for us and our children—and He has a plan to accomplish it.

In this book, we cover simple, foundational truths from God's Word that equip us for the journey (and sometimes fight) of parenting. No matter what we face in this life, we do not fight our battles alone. Like David fighting Goliath, the Lord is on our side (1 Samuel 17). As we teach and train our children in the ways of the Lord, trusting Him through each stage of their development—childhood, adolescence, and adulthood—and engaging with wisdom and diligence, from a biblical worldview, we will see God's Word produce the peaceable fruit of righteousness in their lives. We will see our children shining as lights of God's love and life in the midst of a crooked and perverse generation (Philippians 2:15).

1

Parents as Watchmen

Unless the Lord builds the house, they labor in vain who build it. Unless the Lord guards the city, the watchman stays awake in vain. It is vain for you to rise up early, to sit up late, to eat the bread of sorrows; for so He gives His beloved sleep.

—Psalm 127:1-2

Building a family, like building a house, requires certain skills. It requires foundational truths that only God can provide. God set parents as watchmen over their children. God won't raise children independent of us, and it is extremely unwise for us to raise them independent of Him. We can't do it. We lose sleep and eat the bread of sorrows. But with God's engagement—with His help and instruction—we can fulfill our appointment as parents. We don't need to worry about our children or be filled with anxiety over them. We can cast our care on the Lord (1 Peter 5:7) knowing He empowers us in our parental responsibilities.

God wants us to experience peace as we serve as watchman over our children's lives. The key is balance. Proverbs 11:1 (KJV) says, *"A false balance is an admonition to the Lord: but a just weight is his delight."* We can get in a ditch on either side of the road regarding our ministry as parents and the best method for effective parenting. Some parents are disengaged. They do not understand the importance of being a watchman for their kids. They allow digital media to raise them, and the wolves and lions of this world devour their children.

Others are "helicopter parents." They smother their children, even into adulthood. They try to control them through manipulation and worry. We need to avoid these ditches. Remember, for every mile of road traveled, there is a mile of ditch on both sides. That makes two miles of ditches for every mile of wisdom and understanding. Only through partnership with God and His Word can we remain balanced.

The first thing we need to know to maintain balance is that God loves our kids. His heart is for us and our families. Children are near and dear to God's heart. Yet they are the only thing God did not create independent of man. Think about that. Everything God created He created in maturity. There was no baby Adam or Eve. The first people were created full grown, mature adults who could be *"fruitful and multiply"* (Genesis 1:26-28). It is as if God didn't want to raise teenagers. (I can see the wisdom in that!) Even the promised Messiah came through partnership with man. Mary had to believe before she could receive the promised Seed and bring forth the Holy Child, Jesus (Luke 1:26-38).

Despite this, we see God's love for children throughout scripture. In Matthew 18 the disciples asked Jesus a question:

> *At the same time came the disciples unto Jesus, saying, Who is the greatest in the kingdom of Heaven? And Jesus called a **little child** unto him, and set him in the midst of them, and said, Verily I say unto you, except ye be converted, and become as **little children**, ye shall not enter into the kingdom of heaven. Whosoever therefore shall humble himself as this*

little child, the same is greatest in the kingdom of heaven (Matthew 18:1-4 KJV).

Think about their question: Who is the greatest in God's kingdom? What would we say?

A preacher or TV evangelist with a large following? Maybe a missionary who gave their life on a foreign field? Perhaps they thought Jesus would single out one of them. But the answer Jesus gave likely stunned the disciples. He said the greatest in God's kingdom was a child.

Wow.

Children are full of faith and humility. They are eager to learn; eager to believe. Their imaginations are unparalleled. Children believe animals talk, rabbits lay eggs, and reindeer fly. They believe in Santa Claus, the Tooth Fairy, and Leprechauns—why not the life of Jesus? Jesus' life is much more miraculous than fairy tales. Jesus walked on water. He calmed storms, raised the dead, opened blind eyes, and caused the lame to walk. He fed more than 5,000 people with a little boy's lunch! Our children have faith to believe these marvelous, miraculous acts of God really happened. They can believe Jonah really was swallowed by a big fish; that Daniel spent the night with lions and wasn't eaten; that Moses really split the Red Sea and Elijah called an axe head up from the bottom of a river. Part of our job as watchmen is to protect a child's natural ability to believe.

We are also called to protect our children's moral innocence. In Luke 17:1-2 (NLT), Jesus says to His disciples, *"There will always be temptations to sin, but what sorrow awaits the person who does the tempting! It would be better to be thrown into the sea with a millstone hung around your neck then to cause one of these little ones to fall into sin."* Our culture sets stumbling blocks before children every day. I am appalled at the number of people who are not just inviting children to sin but are taking pleasure in pulling them into sin. I grieve over what they are doing.

Recently, while in Israel, I saw an ancient millstone. Its diameter was nearly as tall as I am! Can you imagine something that size pulling you into the depths of the sea? I cannot think of a more horrific death or a more fitting judgment for harming a child.

As watchmen, we must protect our children from the death and darkness of the world. We must honor God's love for them, for they are special. Their childlike faith reminds us that *all things are possible to those who believe* (Matthew 17:20, 19:26; Mark 9:23). Children encourage us to set aside doubt, to forget about probability or natural law and *"only believe"* (Mark 5:36; Luke 8:50). They inspire us to believe that miracles still happen; that God is the good Father who delights in meeting His children's needs (Romans 8:32-35).

2

A Warrior's Arrows

Behold, children are a heritage from the Lord; the fruit of the womb is a reward. Like arrows in the hand of a warrior, so are the children of one's youth.

—Psalm 127:3-4

Before we break down the illustration of children as arrows, I want to remind us—there are no perfect parents. Neither are there perfect children. We live in a fallen world. But that is exactly why we need God. Without Him, parenthood is a heavy weight, not a reward. Sue and I were not perfect parents; nor did God give us perfect kids. Yet He was faithful to us in the raising of them. And we took comfort in the thought that even God—the perfect Parent—who created two perfect adults, and placed them in a perfect world, did not see perfect results.

As adults, Adam and Eve chose to disobey God's word and plunge the universe into darkness, sin, and death (Genesis 3:1-6; Romans 5:12). Though He was the only innocent party in their sin, God did not forsake them. He loved them. While there were still consequences to Adam's sin, God remained faithful. He promised to send the Deliverer to rescue mankind and bruise Satan's head. God wasn't condemned over His children's actions. And neither should we be condemned if our adult children choose to disobey. God will remain faithful—both to us, as imperfect parents, and to our children. He will not neglect His spoken word or His written Word.

People often ask if I have any regrets over parenthood; would I have done things differently had I known then what I know now. But that's the thing. I didn't know then what I know now. No one does. Sue and I acted in faith then, as we are acting in faith now. And God is blessing us now, as He did then. So, no. We have no regrets. Did we make mistakes? Absolutely! But because we loved God and our children and were faithful to our purpose as parents, God worked all things together for our family's good (Romans 8:28).

Raising children is messy business. But God's grace is sufficient in our human weakness, and He delights in bringing beauty out of ashes (2 Corinthians 12:9; Isaiah 61:3). Trust God to encourage you as you encourage your children in the ways of the Lord. We also hope you'll allow Sue and I to encourage you with this image of children as arrows.

| 0-10 | 10-20 | 20+ |
| (TRAIN) | (TEACH) | (TRANSITION) |

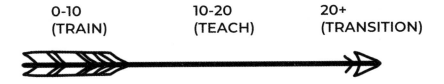

In the construction of an arrow, there are three obvious sections—the tip, the shaft, and the feathers. Each section serves a specific purpose, but all must work together for the arrow to experience success. The same is true of our children. There are three stages in child development (and thus child-rearing) that must work together to successfully launch them into the world—training, teaching, and transition. Our job as parents is to recognize the unique stage our children are in and make the most of every opportunity while they are still in our care (Ephesians 5:15-17).

TIP

GOD'S TARGET IS HIS PURPOSE AND DESTINY FOR THEIR LIFE

The tip of an arrow is designed to hit a specific target. This speaks to the individual destiny of each of our children. Our children were created for a purpose (Jeremiah 29:11). Each has a divine design with gifts and personalities that match God's plan and purpose for their lives. Part of our job as parents is to help them discover those gifts and learn to submit to the leading of the Holy Spirit, so they can take aim at their God-given purpose.

SHAFT

REPRESENTS THE TIME WE HAVE TO PREPARE THEM

The shaft of an arrow determines its length. This correlates to the length of time God gives children into our care—20 years. In that time, we need to train our children to: submit to God (through obedience to us); teach them the ways of the Lord and prepare them for life outside our home; and then transition them into adulthood fully equipped to follow God and succeed in life.

After 20 years, they are adults, responsible and accountable to God for their own decisions and choices.

FEATHERS

THIS REPRESENTS VALUES AND CHARACTER DEVELOPMENT

An arrow's feathers are for accuracy. Feathers guide an arrow through turbulent winds ensuring that the arrow hits its target. Without feathers, an arrow's trajectory is unpredictable. It could harm others or even put itself at risk. This speaks to the spiritual principles we teach our children that guide them through difficult circumstances and keep them rooted in God's love. Without these governing truths, our children will miss God's purpose for their lives. They could also end up harming themselves or others.

Let's look at each of these correlating stages more closely.

STAGES AND AGES

There are three stages of development in every child's life: childhood, adolescence, and adulthood. As parents, our role evolves through these stages. In childhood, we are focused on training and protection. In adolescence, our role shifts to teaching and preparation, and as our children approach adulthood, we transition them out of our care. We become their friend and full-time cheerleader. Before adulthood, we are not our child's friend. We are their guardian and watchmen.

Scripturally speaking, children are considered adults at 20 years of age. In the Bible, 20-year-olds were required to pay the temple tax and go to war with the other adults (Exodus 30:14; Numbers 1:18-42). They were also held accountable for their sin. In Numbers chapter 14, God told the Israelites that those 20 and older would die in the wilderness because they refused to trust Him and enter the Promised Land. The only exceptions were Caleb and Joshua. They did not murmur against the Lord but believed (Numbers 14:29-30). Those under 20 years of age were considered children and not held accountable to God for their sin.

Training

Training is the stage of childhood from zero to approximately 10 years of age. This is the protective stage of parenthood. During this time, we train our children to obey according to Ephesians 6:1-3: *"Children, **obey** your parents in the Lord, for this is right. '**Honor** your father and mother,' which is the first commandment with promise: 'that it may be well with you, and you may live long on the earth.'"* Though there is some teaching that happens in these years, the focus is training our children to obey us, as parents, so that one day they will be able to obey God. Proverbs 22:6 tells us to *"**Train up a child** in the way he should go, and when he is old, he will not depart from it."*

The word *child* is significant in this passage. According to Strong's Concordance, it is the "age of infancy to adolescence" (Strong's H5288). But notice, we are to *train* children. There is a difference between training and teaching. Training involves repetition and consistency. It uses discipline, affirmation, and reward to instill good habits and life skills.

We don't teach lions to jump through hoops or killer whales to perform on demand. We train them. The same is true for children. We don't "teach" life skills once. We train them. (That's why it's called "potty training" not "potty teaching.") From birth to at least eight, we hover over every action and decision our children make. We are helicopter parents. "Don't eat that!" "Don't touch that!" "Don't scratch that!" "Don't pick that!" "Be careful." "Look both ways." "Hold my hand; stay close." We set boundaries for their safety and healthy growth, and when they function within those boundaries, we affirm their choices. "Good job!" "I'm proud of you!" "You are precious." "That was awesome."

We may even offer rewards for their obedience and accomplishments. The key to training is consistency and discipline. What we ask of our children can't be wrong today but okay tomorrow. The consequences of their actions need to be consistent, which means we, as parents, must be diligent. Training children in these early years is a never-ending job. It requires repetitious instruction and demonstration, with lots of patience!

TEACHING

Teaching takes place during adolescence, between the ages of 8 and 10 to 20. This stage of childhood covers the *honor* part of Ephesians 6:2, *"Honor your father and mother, which is the first commandment with promise."* It is the preparation stage in which we teach our children to follow God and live well outside our home.

Proverbs says, *"My son, hear the instruction of your father, and do not forsake the law of your mother. For they will be a graceful ornament on your head and chains about your neck"* (Proverbs 1:8-9). The word *son* is significant in this passage. It is a different Hebrew word from what we saw in Proverbs 22:6. This word means "youth" (Strong's H1121). This is the adolescent stage of childhood. A time is coming when our children will no longer be under our direct authority and will be responsible for their own decisions, but it is not yet. There are things they need to learn first.

The adolescent stage is an important time of teaching and preparation for life. During this time, we prepare our children for marriage, for their future career (not necessarily specific skills, but helping them develop a good work ethic, teaching them to process persecution properly, to get along with unbelievers, etc.), and life in general. We teach them the principles and ways of the Lord, how to be responsible for their actions and accountable before God by focusing on character development, integrity building, and healthy habits so they can be productive adults.

During this time, we explain the *why* of obedience. We teach them how to trust God and submit to His Word in all things because we will not always be there. But what we teach them during this stage will follow them all the days of their lives (Proverbs 4:13 NIV). Even our discipline and correction during adolescence prepares them for the discipline and chastening of the Lord (Hebrews 12:4-11).

TRANSITION

As our children approach age 20, we enter the stage of transition. We have protected them through childhood and prepared them for life outside our home; now, we are to propel them into their future equipped to succeed. By the time our children are 20, we should have resigned from "helicopter parenting" and laid down our role as "teacher." Now we fill the role of friend and counselor (when asked), coach and cheerleader.

By this time, our children should be prepared for adulthood. They should know how to take responsibility for their actions, serve God and their families, and have a good work ethic. They should know they were created on purpose and with a purpose. They should be a giver, not a taker; serving others rather than being a drag on society.

For this stage, they need to know the basics of love—the intentional, God-kind of love that chooses to give freely of itself rather than be served through temporal feelings. This knowledge prepares them to have happy, healthy marriages and to be good parents for the next generation. Titus 2:4 (NLT) tells us that this kind of love is taught, not caught. *"These older women must train the younger women to love their husbands and their children."*

Our children also need to know how to find and fulfill God's will for their life. By 20 they should be trained to seek God's kingdom first and trust that, in Him, all their needs will be met (Matthew 6:33). They should have confidence knowing that God's will for them is only good (Jeremiah 29:11). That no matter what happens, God is for them. He will work all things together for their good because they love Him and are called according to His purpose (Romans 8:28). And they need a solid understanding that transformation and the knowledge of God's will happens through the renewing of their minds (Romans 12:2).

I cannot stress enough the importance of cutting the parental cord during this stage. You have had your children for 20 years. You have sown good seed into their life. You have trained and taught, protected and prepared them to make good choices, be independent, and follow the Spirit's leading. It's time to let them go. Let God take the lead and trust Him to be faithful to His word sown in their hearts.

*"This explains why a **man** leaves his father and mother and is joined to his wife, and the two are united into one"* (Genesis 2:24 NLT; Mark 10:7). This *man* in Hebrew and Greek is an adult. Adults leave

their parents and cleave to their spouses. They get married and sow righteous seeds to create another family who will know what it is to worship and honor God alone. But what about those who don't leave your house to marry or don't marry until later in life? The parental cord of direct authority, oversight, and accountability must still be cut at adulthood, at 20.

Many parents wonder why their adult children avoid them or seem constantly frustrated with them. It might be because the parental cord has not truly been cut. They may fear being manipulated or treated like a child. They could fear your condemnation over their mistakes or your disappointment if they ask for advice then make a different decision. But in our new role as "friend," our children need to know that we trust them to make good decisions or deal with the consequences of their bad ones as an adult. They need to know that we are for them—no matter what, and that we will only give advice when it is asked of us. We must land the helicopter and trust God to guide our children through the next season of their life.

3

GODLY SEED

Didn't the Lord make you one with your wife? In body and spirit you are his. And what does he want? Godly children from your union. So guard your heart; remain loyal to the wife of your youth.

—*Malachi 2:15 NLT*

The most important function of the Christian parent is the raising and rearing of godly seed. This is one of the reasons we get married. According to Malachi, God's plan for man to *"be fruitful and multiply"* was not just to *"replenish the earth"* (Genesis 1:28). God was not just looking for children; He wanted godly children—your children and mine.

It's been said that raising a child takes a village. But that is not true. It takes a dad and mom willing to take on the role of parenthood. I'm not saying no good can come from a single parent household. God's goodness and grace is truly amazing in all our failures and shortcomings (Romans 5:20). What I am saying is that God's best, His optimal plan for our children is to experience the love and care of a father (a male) *and* a mother (a female). A child's success and longevity are connected to knowing both. Fathers are important to a child's development. They speak truth to their children and reinforce their identity.

Mothers are also important. They nurture their children and provide insight into their spiritual and emotional well-being, insight that dads often miss.

Let's refer back to Ephesians 6:1-3: *"Children, obey your parents in the Lord, for this is right. 'Honor your father and mother,' which is the first commandment with promise, 'that it may be well with you, and you may live long on the earth.'"* Notice, this commandment is for children, not adults. The right thing for children to do is obey their parents. But today, society is trying to bypass parents. They want to remove children from their parent's protection. Schools are teaching things without parental knowledge or oversight. Doctors are advocating for treatment without parental consent. This is not right. God gave parents responsibility over their children, not school boards, doctors, or politicians.

I find it interesting that this commandment to children first appeared as part of the Ten Commandments in Exodus 20:12 (NLT). Most people think of the commandments as given to adults. But the New Covenant makes it clear that this command was given to children and given with a promise attached. If obeyed, children could be sure *"to live a long, full life in the land."*

In other words, if children learned to obey and honor their parents they would more easily learn to obey and honor other authorities in life—namely God, but also teachers, police officers, and their future employer—which leads to prosperity, success, and longevity in life. Not that life will be perfect or free of problems. But no matter what our children face, with this attitude of honoring God (learned first by honoring parents), they can prevail. Rebellion, scripture tells us, is like the sin of witchcraft (1 Samuel 15:23). It leads to unnecessary heartache and demonic assault. Obedience leads to long life.

When I worked with my children on honor and obedience I did so out of love for their well-being and concern for their future. I never disciplined them in wrath or with a selfish agenda. I didn't discipline them because I was embarrassed or hurt by their actions. All discipline—from birth to 20 years of age—should be rooted in the child's well-being; for if they learn to honor and obey you, their parents, they will more readily honor and obey God. That is what our discipline is preparing them for—relationship with God.

THE POWER OF PARENTHOOD

Parents, we need to introduce our children to Jesus while they are still young. Scripture teaches that we are to train and teach our children in "the way" of righteousness (Ephesians 6:4; Deuteronomy 32:46-47; Proverbs 12:28). We are not teaching them "a way," nor the world's way. We are instructing them in God's way. We are teaching them righteousness and justice from God's perspective.

Consider why God chose Abraham to be the father of our faith (Genesis 12:1-3). God could have chosen anyone—Abel, Enoch, Noah. But there was something different about Abraham, something that drew God's eye.

> *And the Lord said, "Shall I hide from Abraham what I am doing, since Abraham shall surely become a great and mighty nation and all the nations of the earth shall be blessed in him? For I have known him, in order that he may command his children and his household after him, that they* **keep the way of the Lord, to do righteousness** *and justice, that the Lord may bring to Abraham what He has spoken"* (Genesis 18:17-19).

God knew Abraham. He saw his faith. God knew Abraham would not just maintain his own faith, but he would *"command his children"* and household to keep the way of the Lord. Abraham would protect his children from darkness and introduce them to the Light. He would think generationally.

Now consider Abraham's faith in the offering of Isaac. How was that action proof of Abraham's generational thinking? Abraham knew the gospel. He knew God's Son, the promised Seed, would have to die but that He would also rise again (Galatians 3:8; 1 Corinthians 15:1-4). Abraham knew Isaac was a miracle child, a type of Christ, and he saw the gospel at work through his obedience. Abraham realized that offering Isaac as a sacrifice was a type and shadow of what God would do with His own Son, Jesus. Abraham had no thought of leaving his son dead on that mountain. He even told the servants who journeyed with him, *"Stay here with the donkey; the lad and I will go yonder and worship, and we will come back to you"* (Genesis 22:5).

Abraham knew that if he obeyed God and offered Isaac, God would raise him from the dead.

That is amazing. But perhaps more amazing is Isaac's faith and obedience to his father! It was a three-day journey to Mount Moriah and Isaac had no idea what was in his father's heart; yet he obeyed. When they arrived at the mountain, Isaac said, *"Look, the fire and wood, but where is the lamb for a burnt offering?"* (Genesis 22:7). His father responded, *"My son, God will provide for Himself the lamb for a burnt offering"* (Genesis 22:8). Which, of course, God did, but only after Abraham had built the altar, bound his son, and placed him upon it (Genesis 22:13).

What son stands still while his father binds his hands? What son doesn't struggle or question when his father places him on top of an altar of sacrifice? And what son would stay on that altar as his father raised a knife to take his life? That is faith! And that is the picture of God's love and Jesus' obedience as the sacrificial lamb (Philippians 2:8).

Would your child obey like that? Or would you be chasing them around the mountain? Make no mistake, Abraham had diligently trained and taught Isaac—he had thought and acted generationally—and the fruit of his labor was evident.

Now consider the life of David. King David was a great leader who loved the Lord. But he did not think generationally. He was not a great father. David did not discipline his children, and it cost him (and them) dearly. One of his sons raped a sister (2 Samuel 13:1-21). Another killed his brother in revenge then plotted to overthrow his father's throne (2 Samuel 13:22-29, 15:1-12).

Eli, the high priest in 1 Samuel was of a similar ilk. His sons, Hophni and Phineas, were wicked men who did not honor God or obey their father (1 Samuel 2:12-17). Though they committed abominations in the temple, Eli refused to discipline them, and it did not end well for any of the family (1 Samuel 2:22-25, 30-34). The Lord replaced them with *"a faithful priest who will serve me and do what I desire. I will establish his family, and they will be priests to my anointed kings forever"* (1 Samuel 2:35 NLT).

Thank God for Abraham's obedience in raising a godly seed! Our God is a generational God. He is the God of Abraham, Isaac, and Jacob. And He works generationally. If we are of the faith of Abraham, we too must think generationally. We must watch over our children and household (our children and grandchildren) to teach them the way of the Lord. God has entrusted us with our children. May we be found trustworthy to pass on the faith, to teach them *"the way, truth, and life,"* while they are young and humble of heart, while it is easy to believe (John 14:6). For our children came from God, and they will return to Him through Jesus Christ.

4

RULES

Children, obey your parents in the Lord, for this is right. "Honor your father and mother," which is the first commandment with promise: "that it may be well with you and you may live long on the earth."

—Ephesians 6:1-3

One of the best things we can do for our children is to train them to obey and honor us as parents. God promises if they learn to do that things will go well with them and they will live long on the earth. What parent doesn't want things to go well for their children? The thing is, we don't teach children to obey us and other authorities out of selfishness. Obedience is not an ego trip. "I'm the boss, and you will obey me." Obedience is not supposed to be about us at all. It is about our children and their future.

The three Rs of effective parenting are rules, restraint, and relationship. These things work together, with training in obedience, to impart wisdom to our children and keep them on the path of life.

We can't go anywhere, in life or eternity, where there are no rules. Rules govern school, the workplace, marriage and home, the grocery store, roadways, and the community at large. Even in prison, there are rules.

Think about your favorite sport. Are there not rules that govern its play? Rules keep us safe. They ensure everyone plays the same way and gets a fair shot. But their value goes beyond that. Tennis was an awesome season in my life. Through it, I learned boundaries and submission to authority. I learned self-discipline, the concepts of teamwork and unity, and humility. I learned to respect my opponents and the work they put into the sport, and I learned to respect myself. I learned how to win and lose with grace. These and other life lessons I picked up in tennis still serve me well today. (No pun intended.)

In addition to rules, tennis taught me the value of restraint. Restraints are boundaries. They form the basis of self-control, which every child must learn, and keep us focused and following the right path of life. Self-control serves a child in every area of life. When I was pursuing tennis, even before I returned to the Lord, restraints gave me a measure of success. I practiced for hours every day. I paid attention to what I ate and put into my body because I had a goal, a restraint on my life.

Perhaps the most important element in parenting our children is relationship. Rules without relationship lead to rebellion. But relationship without rules and boundaries is not really relationship, certainly not a healthy one. As parents, we are not just after our children's behavior, we are after their hearts. We want relationship with our children throughout their lives. Once they become adults, the rules that we set over our children will not be the boundary that holds them to the path of life. They need to have their own set of restraints in place. But if we leave relationship out of that process, we'll drive them out of our life and into rebellion. Ultimately, the goal of having relationship with our kids is preparing them for relationship with God.

Parenting Styles

There are four different kinds of parenting—the permissive parent, the overbearing parent, the procrastinating parent, and the relational parent. Permissive parents embody the "live and let live" movement of the 1960s. They never discipline their children but shower them with "love." The problem is their definition of *love*. Proverbs 13:24 says, *"He who spares his rod hates his son, but he who loves him disciplines him promptly."* Love includes discipline. It prioritizes another's good over our comfort.

I don't understand the statement, "I'd rather my child drank and partied in my home than elsewhere." Or, "They're going to have sex anyway, might as well be safe." Why are we encouraging them to drink or have premarital sex at all? That's not going to result in good things. Proverbs 29:15 (AMPC) says, *"The rod and reproof give wisdom, but a child left undisciplined brings his mother to shame."* Our children need discipline to become wise and make wise decisions. Without training, they don't have the ability to consider consequences or recognize how an action will affect their future. They need parents. But not parents who are overbearing.

Often, religious parents fall on this opposite side of the permissive track. They want their child to be wise, they want to protect them, but they are harsh and inflexible. They do not realize that rules and boundaries were created for us, not us for the rules. Ephesians 6:4 (AMPC) says, *"Fathers do not irritate and provoke your children to anger [do not exasperate them to resentment], but rear them [tenderly] in the training and discipline and the counsel and admonition of the Lord."*

Overbearing parents tend to make rules the priority instead of their child's well-being. Some even find joy in punishment. Don't be that parent. Don't push your child away from what is right and just. Don't push them out of relationship or warp their understanding of God's nature.

Remember when the Pharisees questioned Jesus about keeping the Sabbath? They were really concerned about the "rules" connected to keeping the Sabbath, not the disciples' attitude toward relationship with God on the Sabbath. Jesus declared, *"The Sabbath was made for man, and not man for the Sabbath"* (Mark 2:27). Sabbath was not meant to be another rule-filled holy day for the Israelites. It was a reminder to prioritize relationship with God. The Sabbath pointed them to the rest Christ would bring with His death and resurrection. Any rules people observed on that day should have served the purpose of the day—relationship.

Another type of parenting style is procrastination. Procrastinating parents may have good intentions, but they don't do the work necessary to train or teach their children. They think there's always tomorrow. But we only have our children for 20 years. We can't put off parenting them until the teen years. That is not enough time to teach a child everything they need to know to be a successful adult. We have to engage early in our children's lives. We have to teach them to honor God, then transition them over to God's authority and disengage as parents by the time they are 20. We can't wait.

Of course, the balance of all these styles is the relational parent. This parent understands the time. They understand the necessity of rules while prioritizing relationship. And they choose to parent with their child's well-being at heart, not their own comfort, mood, or energy level. These parents are consistent and fair, but also merciful and kind. They respect their children and teach their children to respect others. They recognize that boundaries provide their children with security, so they set up healthy boundaries in which their children can flourish.

The Beauty and Purpose of Rules

Rules exist for our protection. They're not mean, legalistic, or impossible to keep. They don't exist only when someone's in a bad mood. Let's return to the sports analogy. In American football, all players wear helmets. Why? So no one gets a concussion. So no one breaks their neck or crushes their skull. The rule is in place to protect every player. If one player rebels and chooses not to wear a helmet, that player is not going to reach their goal of going to the Super Bowl. They'll not even play. But that decision would have nothing to do with their talent or trustworthiness. It would be because no football team would willingly take on the liability of that player getting injured.

Second Timothy 2:5 says, *"if anyone competes in athletics, he is not crowned unless he competes according to the rules."* The player who does not relate properly to the rules, especially those made to protect and propel them toward their destiny, will not ultimately win. The quicker we teach our kids this lesson, the easier it will be for them to submit to the rules, and the more successful they will be in life.

Outside of obedience, we had two major protection rules when our children were small. "No Touching" and "Stranger Danger." We told them that if someone tried to touch them improperly, specifically in regard to their private body parts, they were to scream bloody murder and let us know immediately. We also told them that they should never get into a car with "a stranger" (but the rule applied to anybody) without our direct permission. If someone came and said, "Your dad or mom sent me to pick you up," they were not to get in that car.

We have since learned the importance of passwords. Passwords work in emergency situations when a parent can't be contacted and the child needs to get a ride from someone. The parent can give that person the password to let the child know they are safe. If you have little children, teach them a safety password that only you and they know. If whomever is trying to pick them up cannot give the child the password, they know to scream and run to safety.

Your family needs rules. Not too many, but enough to provide for their safety and bring a measure of civility and justice to the home. God gave the people of Israel ten rules. Jesus summed them up in one—the "Golden Rule." He says in Matthew 7:12, *"Therefore, whatever you want men to do to you, do also to them, for this is the Law and the Prophets."* Other Bible versions say, *"this sums up the Law and the Prophets."* Teaching our children to think of others will bless every relationship they have. They'll have friends because they're friendly (Proverbs 18:24 KJV). They'll be successful in the workplace because others will want to work with them (Proverbs 16:7). They'll be happily married because of the way they treat their spouse (1 Peter 3:7). They'll also have good relationships with their children and the rest of their family. In short, "treat others the way you wish to be treated," not the way you have been treated or the way you think someone might treat you.

As I said earlier, we find rules in every area of life—in marriage, on the job, in society—and breaking those rules has consequences everywhere we go. If you don't keep the rules in marriage, your marriage will likely end in divorce. If you don't keep the rules related to your career, you'll likely lose your job. If you break the rules of society, you could go to jail. And even there, you'll find rules. Rules aren't confined to this life. Eternity also has rules, just ask Lucifer, or better yet, read what Jesus says in Luke 16:19-23:

> *There was a certain rich man who was clothed in purple and fine linen and fared sumptuously every day. But there was a certain beggar named Lazarus, full of sores, who was laid at his gate, desiring to be fed with the crumbs which fell from the rich man's table. Moreover the dogs came and licked his sores. So it was that the beggar died, and was carried by the angels to Abraham's bosom. The rich man also died and was buried. And being in torments in Hades, he lifted up his eyes and saw Abraham afar off, and Lazarus in his bosom.*

Two men, one rich and one poor, died and entered eternity. One went to hell. The other went to Abraham's bosom, a place of peace and comfort, where the saints of old waited until Jesus came to pay the price for their sins. From hell, the rich man cried out:

> *"Father Abraham, have mercy on me, and send Lazarus that he may dip the tip of his finger in water and cool my tongue; for I am tormented in this flame." But Abraham said, "Son, remember that in your lifetime you received your good things, and likewise Lazarus evil things; but now he is comforted and you are tormented. And besides all this, between us and you there is a great gulf fixed,* **so that those who want to pass from here to you cannot, nor can those from there pass to us**" (Luke 16:24-26).

The rich man asked Abraham to send Lazarus to him with water to ease his torment. Abraham replied, "Umm...can't do that. You had a chance to do right in life, but you chose to live your own way. Now you're going to have to live with the consequences. Besides, there is a huge gulf between us that no one can cross" (my paraphrase).

> *Then he said, "I beg you therefore, father, that you would send him to my father's house, for I have five brothers, that he may testify to them, lest they also come to this place of torment." Abraham said to him, "They have Moses and the prophets; let them hear them." And he said, "No, Father Abraham; but if one goes to them from the dead, they will repent." But he said to him, "If they do not hear Moses and the prophets, neither will they be persuaded though one rise from the dead"* (Luke 16:27-31).

The rich man begged Abraham again, "At least send someone back to warn my family to avoid this place." But Abraham couldn't. There were rules—even in eternity—that could not be broken. So you see, fighting against rules is a losing battle. But learning to relate properly to rules when children are young will help them succeed in life.

The thing we have to remember is that rules serve us; we don't serve the rules. This is often the area Christian parents mess up. They think of rules as another god. They prioritize the rules over the well-being of their child. Scripture deals with this by teaching the balance between the letter and spirit of the law.

We've already mentioned Jesus' response to the Pharisees' question about the Sabbath. Later, He confronted a different set of Pharisees over their tithing practices. *"Woe to you Pharisees! For you tithe mint and rue and all manner of herbs, and pass by justice and the love of God. These you ought to have done, without leaving the others undone"* (Luke 11:42).

These people were giving to be seen of men. They were giving out of obligation, not a heart for God. And they were using their giving as an excuse to not care for their families (Matthew 15:5). Jesus called them out on it. He told them they should do both—obey the letter of the law (the tithe) without neglecting its spirit (to honor their parents).

[God] *made us sufficient as ministers of the new covenant, not of the letter but of the Spirit; for the letter kills, but the Spirit gives life* (2 Corinthians 3:6).

When Jesus answered the Pharisees about their need to keep the Sabbath according to the letter of the Law, He said, *"Have you never read what David did when he was in need and hungry, he and those with him: how he went into the house of God...and ate the showbread, which is not lawful to eat except for the priests...?"* (Mark 2:25-26). This incident happened in 1 Samuel 21. When David was hiding from Saul, he went to the priest in Nob looking for food for himself and his men. The priest had nothing but sanctified bread. But David and his men were starving, so he asked again. Reluctantly, the priest gave him the bread, and years later, God commended David for his actions.

Jesus used David as an illustration of how rules were created for our benefit, not our destruction.

Religion says, "Showbread can only be eaten by a priest." It doesn't take extenuating circumstances into account.

"I know, but I'm dying."

"Sorry. You'll just have to die. We can't break the rules."

But God loves us more than the rules. He says, "Eat the symbol. You are more important."

There was a similar situation in John 8:5-11 when the Pharisees brought a woman caught in adultery to Jesus. This is what happened (paraphrased):

"Moses (the rules) said she should be stoned. What do you say?" the Pharisees asked.

Jesus replied, "If you're without sin, cast the first stone."

One by one the people dropped their stones and left. Then Jesus asked the woman, "Where are your accusers? Has no one condemned you?"

"No one," she replied.

"Then neither do I condemn you; go and sin no more."

Jesus never told the woman her adultery was okay. He told her to go and "sin no more." He called sin what it was, but He didn't condemn her. He could have. Lawfully, He was the only One there who was without sin. But Jesus knew that calling out her sin was a setup. The Pharisees didn't care about the woman or the law. They weren't after justice. If they were, they would have brought the man, too. They wanted to trap Jesus (John 8:6). But Jesus chose mercy.

That is the mastery of parenting— balancing rules with mercy; *I love you* with *Go and sin no more.* As a parent, we must always look at the rules in light of our love for and relationship with our children. Did our child willfully disobey or did they make a childish mistake? Did they fall into temptation or jump in with both feet? Was there malice in their heart? Have they developed a pattern of rebellion or are they just falling short of the standard? Are they repentant? The answer to these questions tells us whether they need consequences or mercy.

If our teenager broke curfew, why? Are they testing the boundaries or is there a legitimate reason they're late? Were they five minutes late once, then ten minutes late the next time? What's going on? Either way, it's time for a conversation. Just remember Micah 6:8: *"He has shown you, O man, what is good; and what does the Lord require of you but to do justly, to love mercy, and to walk humbly with your God?"* As parents, we must always seek what is right and just but continue to love mercy. We must remain humble and open to the Spirit's leading to sow mercy in certain circumstances knowing we, too, need mercy from God.

5

RESTRAINTS

...Christ's love controls us. Since we believe that Christ died for all, we also believe that we have all died to our old life.
—*2 Corinthians 5:14 NLT*

Restraints are external and internal controls in a child's life that teach them God's way of doing things and keep them on the pathway to life. They are like the bumper guards in bowling that keep little ones from getting frustrated when their balls veer into the gutter. Restraints teach our children what is right and keep them in relationship with God when they come out from under our authority.

The first restraint our children should encounter is the love of God. Second Corinthians 5:14 (KJV) tells us that *"the love of Christ constraineth us."* It controls us and keeps us from evil. It keeps us from harming others. Romans 13:10 (KJV) says, *"Love worketh no ill to his neighbour: therefore love is the fulfilling of the law."* Love for God and love for others keeps us from sinning against one another. It is a restraint.

Consequences are another restraint. We should be teaching our children that actions have consequences (cause-and-effect, the law of sowing and reaping) from an early age. When they're young, the rod is an effective consequence. They can't understand the logic behind, "We treat others the way we want to be treated," but they can learn to avoid *Mr. Spoon*. The rod puts a restraint on sin and selfishness.

During adolescence, we use other consequences. By the time our kids are 8 to 10 years old, they can learn through instruction and experience. We can teach them Proverbs 26:27: *"Whoever digs a pit will fall into it, and he who rolls a stone will have it roll back on him."* They can learn from the example of Daniel and Mordecai (Daniel 6; Esther 7). If that doesn't work, they will need to learn by experience.

The school of hard knocks is a good teacher, but the tuition can be high. Teach your children that consequences are a result of the seeds we've sown, not the act of an angry God. Galatians 6:7-8 tells us, *"Do not be deceived, God is not mocked; for whatever a man sows, that he will also reap. For he who sows to his flesh will of the flesh reap corruption, but he who sows to the Spirit will of the Spirit reap everlasting life."* We need to teach our children to repent quickly of the bad seeds they've sown and believe God for crop failure on those seeds. Then, we should teach them how to sow good seeds and expect a good harvest, for God is not mocked. His word is true. We will reap whatever we have sown.

Natural consequences can take time to manifest, however, so as a parent, we often have to invoke logical consequences to ensure our children learn this important life lesson. The key is consistency and clarity. What are the consequences for not making it home on time? Is that fair (can your child control that)? Is it balanced (not too harsh or too lenient)? Be clear about the boundaries you are putting up and be clear about the consequences for stepping outside those boundaries. Make sure the discipline matches the crime. And be consistent. Inconsistency frustrates children.

Reward your child's faithful obedience with age-appropriate privileges. Jesus says, *"He who is faithful in what is least is faithful also in much; and he who is unjust in what is least is unjust also in much,"* and later, to those who were found faithful, He says, *"Well done, good servant; because you were faithful in a very little, have authority over ten cities"* (Luke 16:10; 19:17).

Good parenting rewards faithfulness with extra privileges, and disciplines unfaithfulness with the removal of privileges. This teaches children to own their actions and the consequences of those actions. Just don't get sucked into the modern concept of entitlement. A cell phone is a privilege. A car or time on video games is a privilege. Dating and hanging out with friends are privileges. These things should not be expectations of entitlement. Parents do not "owe" these things to their children, but they can be earned.

Another restraint in our children's lives is vision. Proverbs 29:18 (KJV) says, *"Where there is no vision, the people perish."* The New American Standard version uses the word *unrestrained* instead of *perish*. Our children need a vision for their future. If they leave your home for college without a vision, they will go hog wild (and spend a lot of money unnecessarily). But with a vision, they will use restraint.

As I mentioned, at one time in my life, I had a vision of becoming a professional tennis player. Though I wasn't serving God, this natural vision constrained me. I didn't stay out late or party like others because I always had an upcoming tournament or practice scheduled. That natural vision benefited me for a season—but think what a godly vision would have done. In fact, in

May 1980, I had an open vision of the Cross. I saw the extent of Jesus' love for me and my identification with Him in death and resurrection. That godly vision has constrained my life to this day!

We need to make sure our kids have a vision for their future. If not a career vision, then one of marriage and family; one of a healthy life. That vision will be like borders to their life. It will put a restraint on their actions.

Your influence as a godly parent is also a restraint in your child's life. Ephesians 6:1 says, *"Children, obey your parents in the Lord, for this is right."* Do you know the story that we touched on briefly of Eli, the high priest? Eli had two sons. Like all Levites, his sons were tasked with caring for the tabernacle. But they were wicked men. They did not follow the Lord and abused their position. They ate the people's sacrifices and had sex with female worshippers at the tabernacle door. Their father knew what was going on, but he did not discipline them. First Samuel says that God confronted Eli about this lapse. *"For I have told him that I will judge his house forever for the iniquity which he knows, because his sons made themselves vile, and he did not restrain them"* (1 Samuel 3:13).

It is one thing for our children to make a mistake, but another for them to habitually sin and us to do nothing about it. Parents are called to be a godly restraint in their children's lives. "But" people cry, "if I try to restrain them, they might hate me." If you do not restrain them, they will surely hate you and may eventually die. On the other hand, Hebrews says those who are disciplined in love learn to respect their parents (Hebrews 12:9).

Proverbs 13:24 says, *"He who spares his rod hates his son, but he who loves him disciplines him promptly."* Discipline (or avoiding discipline) is not about a child hating you, it's about you hating them. According to scripture, withholding discipline is hatred.

Spiritual authorities can also be a restraint in our children's lives. Good children's church and youth pastors are allies in parenting, not adversaries. Hebrews 13:7 and 17 say, *"Remember those who rule over you, who have spoken the word of God to you, whose faith follow, considering the outcome of their conduct. ...Obey those who rule over you, and be submissive, for they watch out for your souls, as those who must give account. Let them do so with joy and not with grief, for that would be unprofitable for you."*

The key is to *"know those who labor among you"* and choose the influences in your child's life wisely (1 Thessalonians 5:12). Aaron was supposed to serve as a restraint for God's people when Moses went up the mountain to receive the Ten Commandments. But he didn't. He allowed the people to run wild. They convinced him to make an idol for them so they could prostitute themselves before it.

"And when Moses saw that the people were unruly and unrestrained (for Aaron had let them get out of control, so that they were a derision and object of shame among their enemies)" (Exodus 32:25 AMPC). Before Moses could come down the mountain with God's law, the people sat at the bottom breaking all ten rules. And Aaron went right along with them. He didn't want to be the "bad guy" and tell the Israelites, "No." The devil used this weakness in Aaron to try and destroy God's people before Moses could tell them the boundaries that would save their lives.

God's Word also creates boundaries for us to live by. Psalm 119:11 (KJV) says, *"Thy word have I hid in mine heart that I might not sin against thee."* The word of God is supernatural. It causes us to stop sinning against Him. That's why it's so important to get God's Word in your children's hearts while they are young. (And why the devil hates the Bible so much.) It is a restraint against evil. Man, without God, wants to act without consequences, guilt, or judgment. He wants restraints removed. The psalmist, in Psalm 2:1,3-4, asks, *"Why do the nations rage and the people plot a vain thing? ...Let us break their bonds in pieces and cast away their cords from us." He who sits in the heavens shall laugh...."* The Amplified Classic Bible version says, *"Let us break Their bands [of restraint] asunder and cast Their cords [of control] from us"* (Psalm 2:3).

While man is free to sin and rebel against God, that path always leads to unhappiness, destruction, and death. The Word of God makes known to us the path of life (Psalm 16:11). It keeps our consciences sensitive by letting us know right from wrong. The more time we spend in God's Word and in fellowship with other believers at a church where the Spirit of God is moving, that clarity gets louder. Jesus says, *"Sanctify them by Your truth. Your word is truth"* (John 17:17). And again, *"If you abide in My word, you are My disciples indeed. And you shall know the truth, and the truth shall make you free"* (John 8:31-32). Holiness is not a work of the flesh or self-effort. It is a by-product of God's Word hidden in our hearts.

When our children were young, they learned the ABCs to scripture. They learned:

A – All have sinned and come short of the glory of God (Romans 3:23 KJV)

B – Believe on the Lord Jesus Christ and thou shall be saved (Acts 16:31 KJV)

C – Children, obey your parents in the Lord, for this is right (Ephesians 6:1)

D – Depart from evil and do good (Psalm 34:14)

E – Even a child is known by his doings (Proverbs 20:11 KJV), and so on.

The Word of God sown in their heart was a restraint against evil. It worked like seed planted in a garden and has produced a harvest of righteousness in both their and their children's lives. Can you imagine the benefits of that much scripture planted in your child's heart by the time he or she is five or six years old? Powerful!

The body of Christ, the church, can also serve as a restraint for our children. Paul told Timothy, a young pastor, *"If I am delayed, I write so that you may know how you ought to conduct yourself in the house of God, which is the church of the living God, the pillar and ground of the truth"* (1 Timothy 3:15). The church is where we get grounded in the truth. It provides a covering and safety net for every believer, a place of refuge from the darkness of this world, and a place of support and encouragement for families.

Matthew 5:13-14 compares the church to salt and light. *"You are the salt of the earth....You are the light of the world. A city that is set on a hill cannot be hidden."* Salt preserves and protects meat from spoilage, while light exposes and expels darkness. A city set on a hill can be seen from miles around, but it is also protected from invasion and enemy assaults. Do we not want such protection in our lives? In our family's lives? Then we need to be in church.

Our children need to understand who they are as members of the body of Christ on earth. When we, the people of God, gather in faith, we become a sanctuary for the lost and hurting in our world. But we must keep assembling as the Church and exhorting one another with this truth.

And let us consider one another in order to stir up love and good works, not forsaking the assembling of ourselves together, as is the manner of some, but exhorting one another, and so much the more as you see the Day approaching (Hebrews 10:24-25).

Good church culture is vital to God's plan in the last days. When we gather, we provoke one another toward love and good works. We encourage one another and keep ourselves from being spoiled by this world. We put a restraint on sin. When we come together and unite in a common goal and purpose around the Lord Jesus Christ, His word, and the work and move of the Holy Spirit, we become a city set on a hill. There is just something about being in church that offers a measure of protection in our lives. I'm not saying if you go to church, you won't sin, but boy, it's a lot harder than if you aren't in church. Get your children in a good church and get them involved. It will be a restraint on sin and a place for them to develop good relationships.

6

Relationship

Do not be deceived: "Bad company corrupts good character."
—*1 Corinthians 15:33 Berean Standard Bible*

The final R in good parenting is relationship. Relationship is the lynchpin that makes all other skills work. That's why we don't respond well to rejection. We were created for love. We were created for relationship with God (Ephesians 1:5-6). Without relationships, life is worthless, family is dysfunctional, and religion is dead. Pure Christianity is not just another religion with a different or better set of rules. It is relationship with the true and living God in the Person of the Lord Jesus by the agency of the Holy Spirit and in accordance with God's Word (John 17:3; Jeremiah 31:34; Hebrews 8:11-12). The first place we learn this is in our family.

Faith is the greatest legacy we can leave our children and grandchildren. Faith trusts God's love and care. It believes in His goodness and goodwill toward us and is our positive response to His grace. This is the importance of family and godly friends (and the goal of our parenting)—to provide a tangible demonstration of God's love toward our children and introduce them to the meaning of relationship with God.

We need to share our faith with our children in practical ways while they are still young. During their early years, it is easy for them to believe. It's easy for them to believe in the miracles of Jesus and the Old Testament saints. It is easy for them to believe that since God protected the three Hebrew children in the fiery furnace, He will protect them. We need to share biblical stories and the miracles of Jesus—especially the resurrection—with our kids while they are young. And when they believe—when they understand faith in Jesus as Lord and accept God's gift of salvation—we need to celebrate with them.

Sue and I were very purposeful in this area. We did not want our children to enter adulthood thinking they could no longer believe the impossible. We wanted them to believe in the miraculous, so we told them the truth about Santa Claus and the Easter bunny from the beginning. We knew that if they grew up believing those things were real then later learned it was a lie, they would also question the truth of the Bible. We wanted them to believe the truth from a young age and never lose it.

Getting God's Word into our children's hearts produces a harvest of righteousness and an explosion of faith over time—and it starts in the family. Paul recognized this in the life of Timothy when he writes, *"I call to remembrance the genuine faith that is in you, which dwelt first in your grandmother Lois and your mother Eunice, and I am persuaded is in you also"* (2 Timothy 1:5).

Everything God does is about family. We are part of the family of God (Ephesians 3:15). He is called our heavenly Father (Matthew 6:9). Jesus is the Son of God sent to save us (John 3:16).

We are called brothers and sisters in Christ (Mark 3:35). *"God sets the solitary in families; He brings out those who are bound into prosperity…"* (Psalm 68:6). Healthy families contribute to healthy churches that build healthy communities. Even the collapse of our culture can be traced back to the destruction of the family.

Our children need their family. They need a dad and a mom. They need extended family to love them and model the love of God for them and one another.

The relationships our children build with friends is important, too. Scripture declares, *"Do not be deceived: 'Evil company corrupts good habits'"* (1 Corinthians 15:33). The friends our children choose will become their future. And while we cannot choose their friends for them, we can approve or disapprove of their choices.

Friends, especially during the teenage years, are second only to us in the influence they have in our children's lives and choices. If we are wise, we will admonish our children to choose wisely in this regard. Proverbs 13:20 (MSG) says, *"Become wise by walking with the wise; hang out with fools and watch your life fall to pieces."* Don't be deceived, the negative influence of friends can corrupt all the good you pour into your child. In our house, we had this rule: If you are influencing your friend for good, you can continue to hang out; but if your friend is influencing you for bad, we will have to reverse course.

Never underestimate the power of friendship. Never say to your child, "If your friend jumps off a bridge, would you?" Of course they will! It is very important to know your child's friends, and not just by name. Know who they are, know their character, and watch for their positive or negative influence on your child. The home court advantage is the best way to do this. Have your child's friends over to your house as often as possible. Let your home be the number-one hangout. (And put the pizza delivery guy on speed dial!) Eating together as a family. But don't be afraid to occasionally include their friends. You'd be amazed how much relationship is built around a table.

I understand that culture has changed. People are busy, and it can be hard to plan regular time together. But that just underscores the importance of being active in the building of relationships within and without the family unit. My daughters were a little more difficult for me to build relationship with than my sons. The boys and I were close. We enjoyed the same things. But when the girls came along, I had to work harder. I had to do things I didn't necessarily enjoy, like shopping. However, I discovered that in shopping they would talk about things they normally didn't talk about with me. All because I took the time to show them how important they were. That's what relationship is all about. Spending time together proved my love for them. It helped them see that I was *for* them, and helped them remember that, even in discipline.

People say it's quality time that counts with kids, not quantity. While I agree that quality time is important, there can be no quality of time independent of quantity. Children need both. I took all four of my children on the road with me at different times when I traveled. During those years, I was a pseudo-homeschooling parent, which allowed me to obey the call of God on my life without damaging my family relationships.

We have to make time for our kids. We can't build relationship through one to three sentence texts. *Hurry* and *busy* are the enemies of intimacy. So, take time to do things as a family. Vacation and road trip together. Vacations facilitate time and conversation. And they're fun! We tend to open up when we're having fun. Even when things break down or fall apart (which happens to everyone), memories are built during these "get aways." Road trips build relationship with your kids and provide times of fellowship that just don't happen at home. Where else will you create the "Do you remember..." stories?

Do things your kids enjoy. Celebrate birthdays. Plan special holiday meals. Go fishing or hunting or camping. Ride rollercoasters together. These moments deposit relational capital into your child's heart. And that capital sustains them when life is hard. It protects them when love has to be tough (Colossians 3:14). And most importantly, it opens their heart to relationship with God. Nothing could be more precious than that.

7

Good Communication

Let your conversation be always full of grace, seasoned with salt, so that you may know how to answer everyone.
  —*Colossians 4:6 NIV*

Mankind was created for fellowship, for relationships. But our level of relationship is directly connected to our ability to foster good communication. Communication is everything. And praise God, it is a learned skill! Paul lays out a few of the necessary elements of communication in Colossians when he says, *"Let your conversation be always full of grace, seasoned with salt, so that you may know how to answer everyone"* (Colossians 4:6 NIV). Families need to learn to speak to one another in grace. Words have power. As parents, we are to model gracious words to our children. We are to speak life over them and learn to listen to them. Listening is more than just hearing. Listening involves understanding. Without it, we cannot know how to answer in truth.

The elements of communication—talking and listening—build relationship between the communicators. But another element is needed for our communication to be effective, and that is feedback. I know it sounds elementary, but we can't communicate without talking. Notice I said talking, not lecturing. Good parents talk with their children. They have dialogue. Monologues, or one-sided talking with no expectation of a response, are not part of effective communication. Neither is shouting, arguing, or verbal attacks. As parents, we can't take the easy route and fall into the habit of monologue-correcting or teaching our child. We need to talk *with* our children, not *at* them.

Parents, this may be news to you, but we are the adults in the relationship with our children. We are responsible for controlling the tone, attitude, and level of conversation our family engages in. We are the models. Our example will either raise our child's communication skills to become mature, civil conversation participants or trap them into immaturity.

Listening is another component to good communication. As a whole, our culture does not know how to listen. James 1:19-20 (NLT) says, *"Understand this, my dear brothers and sisters: You must all be quick to listen, slow to speak, and slow to get angry. Human anger does not produce the righteousness God desires."* As parents, we need to be quick to listen. We need to learn our child's verbal and non-verbal language and give them the opportunity to use it.

Unfortunately, most parents, especially dads, have a tendency to interrupt their children's stories and try to fix whatever issue they are dealing with. I learned the hard way that often our kids aren't asking us to fix their problems. They just need someone to process them with; they need us to understand.

During adolescence, my girls taught me to "nod my head and act spiritual." They would start telling me about their day, and I would want to interrupt. "You know, if you hadn't done that or said this, the issue wouldn't have happened in the first place. But since you did, here's how to fix it." Then I'd get *the look*. Every guy knows what I'm talking about—that piercing look only women have. And when you see it, you know you're in trouble.

My girls would look at me and say, "Dad, can I just finish the story?" They didn't want my advice. They wanted my understanding. They wanted relationship. The good news is my understanding did not mean I had to agree with or like what they told me. I just had to nod my head and act spiritual.

The other thing I had to learn as I communicated with my children was to shut down the temptation to top their story. They might be telling me about something bad that happened at school and I would want to interrupt with something bad from my day, just to help them put their "pain" into perspective. Maybe your parents did this. Maybe they said things like, "Well, when I was young, I had to walk to school in the snow. Uphill. Both ways. With no shoes on." We all need to get over that. Story comparison is not part of effective communication. We must learn to listen, to lean in and hear what our children are really saying. That's what scripture is talking about when it admonishes us to be quick to listen and slow to speak (James 1:19).

The best way I know to do this is to get feedback. I know feedback can feel awkward and uncomfortable at first, but you'd be surprised how many things we miss without this skill. Jesus often told His listeners, *"He who has an ear, let him hear what the Spirit says."* Everyone has ears, but not everyone hears what is being said. In other words, we have to choose to listen and seek to understand.

Our brains are amazing. They hear and see and feel everything. But they can also wipe out unimportant stimuli. Without that ability, we'd go crazy. Have you ever been at a restaurant when a conversation at the table next to you suddenly catches your attention? The people at that table were probably talking the whole time, but until you chose to hear, you didn't hear.

What about right now? If you stopped reading for a second and chose to hear what was going on around you, what sounds would you hear? This choice, this decision to hear, is vital to our communication patterns. But how do we know others have chosen to hear? Feedback. Without receiving feedback, we can't know if what we've said is heard and understood by whomever we're speaking to. And without giving feedback, we can't know if what we've heard is what was actually intended.

I remember leaving the house in a hurry once years ago. I hollered at my oldest son as I walked out the door. "Jeremy, make sure you cut the grass!"

"Sure, Dad."

But when I came home, the grass was not cut. And I was not a happy camper. "Son, why is the grass not cut?"

"I don't know, Dad."

"What do you mean you don't know?"

"I don't know."

"I told you to cut the grass, Jeremy, and you said, 'Sure, Dad.' So, why isn't it cut?"

"Oh…I thought you said never *smoke* grass. Sorry, Dad."

It's funny now, but I wasn't really thrilled then. Had I stopped to get feedback, this episode wouldn't have happened. If Jeremy had responded with, "Sure, Dad. I remember what you taught me. I'll never smoke grass." I would have said, "I appreciate that, but you misheard me. I want you to *cut* the grass." See? Feedback.

But remember, this feedback thing goes both ways. We need to get feedback when we instruct our children, and we need to give feedback when they communicate with us to make sure we are all hearing correctly and understanding what is being said. If you haven't already set up a feedback loop with your family, start one today. Feedback is simple. It reiterates what was said, what was heard, and what was meant. Feedback asks questions to gain clarity and is the first step toward resolving miscommunication.

"Okay. But how does that help when my kids won't talk to me?" Initiate conversation. Don't wait for or expect your children to start this process. Go the extra mile. Our kids are still developing their communication skills, and as they are learning, they can sometimes digress. When they're young, it takes almost no effort to get our children to spend time with us and talk to us. As teenagers, a lot more is happening under the surface. It feels easier for them to hide in their phones or video games than to do the hard work of processing their thoughts and feelings.

But stay engaged. Spend time with them. Keep pressing. Keep pushing. Keep asking questions (Proverbs 20:5 NLT). Keep pursuing the things they enjoy. Choose strategic moments to talk with your kids and give them the opportunity to communicate. Pick them up from school. Take them out on dates. Hunting was always where my kids and I bonded. It's amazing what they would talk to me about while we were sitting in a deer stand. So keep talking with your kids and give them time to talk with you.

There is no substitute for time. Spend time together as a family. Eat meals together as often as possible. Go to church together. Take vacations together. Have fun as a family and talk. Talk to your kids about their favorite band, their best friend, their favorite sports team(s). Then tell them about yours. Ask your kids about their favorite TV show or movie, their favorite place to eat out, their least favorite class at school. Talking with your kids about the things they are passionate about opens those doors of communication and makes it easier for them to talk about deeper things, like what scares them or what they're struggling with.

No matter what you talk to your children about, empathize with them. Put yourself in their place. Remember what it was like to face the pressures of school, the temptation to conform, the drama of friendship. Remember the anxiety you felt when trying to figure out what to do after graduation? And remember, they do not have the life experience you do. They haven't learned how to draw on the power of God like you have, so empathize with them. Don't dump on them when they are hurting or stressed. Listen to them. Pray with them. And help them separate their actions or feelings from their identity.

To do that, you have to be able to separate your own performance, as a parent or otherwise, from your identity. If you get defensive or feel discouraged when someone corrects or critiques you on the job or at home, you have not yet learned to separate your identity from your performance. Many believers do not know how to do this. When they make a mistake, they think they are a mistake. When they fail, they think they are a failure. That is not true. Quit doing that. You are a child of God. If, in a weakness, you have failed—repent. That's not who you are anymore. In Christ, you are righteous and truly holy (Ephesians 4:24). You are not a failure, you are now an overcomer in Christ. Act like who you are. Separate your actions from your identity and begin to see yourself as God sees you.

I taught my kids that they were a ten in Christ. They were the head, not the tail; above, not beneath (Deuteronomy 28:13). I taught them that they had the power to change the world. Even when they messed up, I told them, "I love you unconditionally. I'll never quit loving you. I'll never give up on you. I'm committed to your good. What you did was unacceptable, but that doesn't change who you are." I helped them separate who they were from what they did.

You, too, are a ten in the eyes of God. That doesn't mean you won't mess up. Sometimes, we all do a piece of stupid, yet God loves us. He doesn't give up on us. We're His kids and as long as we stay humble—believing what He says above what we feel—we'll keep growing in our knowing of who we are in Christ and our flesh will conform to that image (Romans 8:29). It's a process. But God sees the end from the beginning (Isaiah 46:10). Just because we're still in the process doesn't mean we aren't valuable to and loved by Him.

Our kids need to see this truth reflected in our relationship with them. Our oldest daughter is one of our most dramatic children. Raising her was a ride! Most times, it was an absolute joy; other times, I thought I was losing my mind. But man, I love her! She taught me a lot about myself.

When she was about five, I had to discipline her for disobedience, and she fell apart. "I'm just so bad!" she cried. "I'm going to die and go to hell."

"No, baby," I said. "You're not bad. What you did was bad. You're very good; now act like it."

A few months later, she was in trouble again. "I don't know if I can obey," she wailed. "I just want to die and go to heaven."

Her revelation was progressing. But she still needed help separating her identity from her performance. Your kids will probably need help with that, too. Philemon 1:6 says that our faith works by acknowledging the good things in us in Christ. If we want our kids' faith to work, they have to know who they are in Christ. They have to be able to separate their performance from their identity. It's fine to address weakness in our children, but we also need to help them recognize their strength in Christ to overcome that weakness.

One of the most overlooked areas of communication in adults and children alike is tone. The tone of our voices often speaks louder than our words. So, speak kindly to your children. Control your emotions. If you expect your child to control their attitude with you, you cannot be just as quick to get emotional with them. What does that say to them? At certain points in their lives, children will *try* to push your buttons. They want to see if you really believe what you're preaching. In all things, hold tight to Ephesians 4:29 (NLT): *"Don't use foul or abusive language. Let everything you say be good and helpful, so that your words will be an encouragement to those who hear them."* Be a good example, and remember that facial expressions count, too.

I remember driving my kids home from school years ago. My oldest daughter was only about six or seven and just jabbering away. Perhaps I wasn't responding as vocally as I should have, but she suddenly reached over and grabbed my face. She turns it toward herself (while I was still driving) and said, "Look at me when I'm talking to you." I had taught her to look at me when I talked to her.

Well, that didn't fly. I tried to explain to her that I had to pay attention to the road, but she didn't understand. She wanted my attention on her.

"Are you mad at me?" she asked.

"No, I'm not mad at you."

"Are you sure you're not mad at me?"

"I'm sure, I'm not mad. But I have to drive right now."

"I think you are mad."

"I'm not mad." But boy was I getting there!

Matthew 6:22-23 says, *"The lamp of the body is the eye. If therefore your eye is good, your whole body will be full of light. But if your eye is bad, your whole body will be full of darkness...."* Our eyes are windows into our soul; they direct our focus. As much as possible, look at your children when you're talking to them or they are talking to you, and teach them to do the same. Show them that they are your focus. And be fully present (unless you're driving) during conversations with them. Don't let them drift. This little skill will drastically improve your family's communication.

8

A Legacy of Faith

> *Now may the God of peace Himself sanctify you completely; and may your whole spirit, soul, and body be preserved blameless at the coming of our Lord Jesus Christ. He who calls you is faithful, who also will do it.*
>
> —*1 Thessalonians 5:23-24*

The greatest legacy we can leave our children and grandchildren is faith. Faith in the one true God. Faith in His love and the provision He made for us in salvation through Jesus. Faith in the resurrection and our Lord's return. And believe it or not, everything we do for and with our children points them toward or away from that faith. God cares about every part of our lives—spirit, soul, and body. All three play a role in His will for us, and He works in partnership with us in each area. As parents, we must be vigilant in the raising of our children to protect them in all three areas and to teach them how to partner with God in each one.

We can look after the spiritual health of our children by imparting these basic spiritual truths to them:

Our need for God:

For all have sinned and come short of the glory of God (Romans 3:23).

GOD'S LOVE FOR US ALL:

For God so loved the world that He gave His only begotten Son, that whoever believes in Him should not perish but have everlasting life (John 3:16).

Yes, I have loved you with an everlasting love; therefore with lovingkindness I have drawn you (Jeremiah 31:3).

HOW TO BE BORN AGAIN:

For by grace you have been saved through faith, and that not of yourselves; it is the gift of God (Ephesians 2:8).

If you confess with your mouth the Lord Jesus and believe in your heart that God has raised Him from the dead, you will be saved (Romans 10:9).

Jesus answered, "Most assuredly, I say to you, unless one is born of water and the Spirit, he cannot enter the kingdom of God. That which is born of the flesh is flesh, and that which is born of the Spirit is spirit. Do not marvel that I said to you, 'You must be born again" (John 3:5-7).

OUR NEW IDENTITY IN CHRIST:

Therefore, if anyone is in Christ, he is a new creation; old things have passed away; behold, all things have become new (2 Corinthians 5:17).

For He made Him who knew no sin to be sin for us, that we might become the righteousness of God in Him (2 Corinthians 5:21).

For if by the one man's offense death reigned through the one, much more those who receive abundance of grace and of the gift of righteousness will reign in life through the One, Jesus Christ. ...For as by one man's disobedience many were made sinners, so also by one Man's obedience many will be made righteous (Romans 5:17,19).

THE FEAR OF AND REVERENCE FOR GOD:

The fear of the Lord is the beginning of knowledge (Proverbs 1:7).

Give unto the Lord the glory due to His name; worship the Lord in the beauty of holiness (Psalm 29:2).

We also need to watch over the health of our children's souls. We need to teach them critical thinking skills. We cannot allow the world to shape their view of right and wrong, good and evil. We cannot allow the world to warp their view of God. We need to teach our kids how to think and process information. We need to teach them truth. *"The entirety of Your word is truth, and every one of Your righteous judgments endures forever"* (Psalm 119:160). Jesus prayed, *"Sanctify them by Your truth. Your word is truth"* (John 17:17).

This world would have our children be conformed into any image but Christ. As parents, we combat this by teaching them the difference between carnal and spiritual thinking and sharing

God's thoughts on every subject with them (Romans 8:6; 12:2). Without that understanding, the philosophy of the current culture will spoil our children. *"Don't let anyone capture you with empty philosophies and high-sounding nonsense that come from human thinking and from the spiritual powers of this world, rather than from Christ"* (Colossians 2:8 NLT).

How many good Christian parents do not take this charge seriously? They allow their children to leave their home unprepared for the philosophies, vain deceit, and demonically inspired lies of this world. In college, our children are told the Bible is just a book; it's not God's Word. They're told faith is unreasonable, morals are subjective, and truth is relative. They're taught that abortion is right and just, a fix for global warming and population control. They're taught that sex is love, work is slavery, and capitalism evil. They're taught to trust the media, trust "science," and trust the government to provide all their needs. These, and many other lions of culture, wait outside your home. Do not let them devour your children!

Your kids are your responsibility to teach and train. They are under your covering until the age of 20. We cannot send our kids out of our house and into the lion's den of this world for two to four years and be surprised when they come back with a corrupted soul—renouncing their faith, rejecting God's Word, and embracing the things God commands us to reject. They're not adults yet. What if, instead, we sent them to Bible school for two years after they graduated high school? They could sit under the Word of God for hours every day and develop a biblical worldview, a godly philosophy. Our kids need to learn to set their minds on things above so they can discern what is truly just and right and equitable (Colossians 3:1-4).

We have to guard our children's heart—their soul—for out of it flows the issues of life (Proverbs 4:23). By 20, our children will be out of our house; they will be out from under our covering and accountable to God. Let's make sure they are prepared.

The last area of life we must protect our children and teach them to partner with God is in their bodies. Romans 12 says:

> I beseech you therefore, brethren, by the mercies of God, that you present your **bodies a living sacrifice**, holy, acceptable to God, which is your reasonable service. And do not be conformed to this world, but be transformed by the renewing of your mind, that you may prove what is that good and acceptable and perfect will of God (Romans 12:1-2).

As a whole, the Church has not done a good job teaching believers to discipline their bodies without getting legalistic; and so, we are more conformed to the world in this area than transformed by Christ. We are sick. We overindulge in food and drink (then look to the world for easy fixes). We're in debt. We are profoundly affected by sex. We think like, look like, and talk like the world. But our bodies are not our own. They belong to God and our future mate. First Corinthians 6:15,19-20 says:

> Do you not know that your bodies are members of Christ? Shall I then take the members of Christ and make them members of a harlot? Certainly not! ...Or do you not know that your body is the **temple of the Holy Spirit** who is in you, whom you have from God, and you are not your own? For you were bought at a price; therefore glorify God in your body and in your spirit, which are God's.

Our kids are being told they have a right to their bodies (unless it's Covid). Yet, according to scripture, we can't experience the good, acceptable, and perfect will of God independent of our bodies being dedicated to Him and our minds renewed to His Word. Paul says, *"I keep under my body and bring it into subjection lest by any means, when I've preached to others, I myself should be a castaway"* (1 Corinthians 9:27 KJV). In other words, we have to rule our bodies, our emotions and feelings, and bring them into subjection so our bodies don't rule us. Do our kids know that? Do they know we can hinder God's will in our lives by not yielding our bodies to Him?

We must learn for ourselves and teach our children to rule over and discipline their bodies. We must rule over hunger, rule over thirst. We must rule over the desire for stuff. We must rule over our sexuality, or we will become a castaway. *Castaway* means worthless, rejected, and reprobate (Strong's G96). Our sexuality is a gift from God reserved for marriage. It is a healthy drive, but it can't rule over us.

First Corinthians reports on a man in the church who was sleeping with his stepmother, a practice strictly forbidden by God. The church was aware of this man's sin, but they did not correct him. They did not even mourn his actions. Rather they boasted about their tolerance and celebrated the grace that excused his sin (1 Corinthians 5). They were deceived. Paul says, *"Your glorying is not good. Don't you know a little leaven, a little sin, leavens the whole lump?"* (1 Corinthians 5:6, paraphrased).

I know there's a lot of confusion over the New Testament believer's relationship with the law. But what was the purpose of the law? To reveal sin; to express God's standard of morality and show us our utter lack of it (Romans 7:13). The law was given to drive us to Christ. But God's standard of morality didn't change with the law. It has always been constant. Adultery was wrong before God gave the law to Moses. It was wrong under the law. And it is still wrong today. Jesus didn't come to remove morality. He didn't come to abolish the law; He came to fulfill it so we could have relationship with God (Matthew 5:17).

Jesus removed the curse associated with breaking the law (Galatians 3:13). Now, as a New Testament believer, I am not under the law with all its rituals, sacrifices, feasts, new moons, and sabbaths. Those things point to Jesus. I am under *grace* and His command to love (Romans 13:8-10). That doesn't mean I am lawless. Love for God and others fulfills the law in my life; it constrains me from within (Romans 5:5; 2 Corinthians 5:14). Because I love God, I do what is right and moral. Because I love my wife and kids, I do not commit adultery.

The world tells our children, "Do what makes you happy" (meaning, whatever pleases the flesh). And if they stand up for what is right and moral, the world will say, "Don't judge me!" But Jesus never said, "Do not judge." Instead, He taught us *how* to judge. He said, *"Do not judge according to appearance, but judge with righteous judgment"* (John 7:24). How do we know what is righteous? We look to God's standard of morality. For though we are not to pass final judgment on anyone—that's God's role—we are to warn sinners of the judgment to come. We are to condemn the things God has already judged so the one trapped in sin can repent (Romans 10:14-15).

We all need forgiveness. We all need mercy. So, we should judge accordingly. We should not condemn our children for failing or falling in any area, but neither can we condone what God condemns (Galatians 6:1). We must teach our children to control their bodies, especially in sexual purity, so they can control them after marriage (1 Thessalonians 4:3; 1 Corinthians 6–7).

> *And so, dear brothers and sisters, I plead with you to give your bodies to God because of all he has done for you. Let them be a living and holy sacrifice—the kind he will find acceptable. This is truly the way to worship him* (Romans 12:1 NLT)

Paul could judge the situation in 1 Corinthians with boldness because he knew what God's Word said about sexual immorality. Paul evoked church discipline to protect the other members of the body. He also hoped it would save the man's soul (1 Corinthians 5:4-9). Our children need to understand that while God does not pour out wrath and curses if we fail, sin is still deadly. It has consequences. And while God judges those outside His church, we are called to judge those within—especially ourselves and those within our homes, from birth to age 20 (1 Corinthians 5:10-12; Matthew 7:1-5).

Training

Train up a child in the way he should go and when he is old, he will not depart from it.

—*Proverbs 22:6*

9

EVERY CHILD'S GREATEST NEED

Satisfy us each morning with your unfailing love, so we may sing for joy to the end of our lives.

—Psalm 90:14 NLT

A lot of things have changed in this generation. Our children and grandchildren have access to an astounding amount of information, yet there is a drought of wisdom. But with all this information, mankind has not changed. Our problems and challenges are still the same. Humans are anxious and stressed. Fearful. Self-righteous. We spend our lives seeking new and creative solutions to our problems while ignoring the heart condition that created those challenges in the first place. Ecclesiastes says, *"…The eye is not satisfied with seeing, nor the ear filled with hearing. That which has been is what will be, that which is done is what will be done, and there is nothing new under the sun"* (Ecclesiastes 1:8-9).

The eye will never be satisfied until it sees God and His love for us. The ear will never hear a philosophy of the world that brings peace. Only God's love can satisfy. First John 2:16 says, *"For all that is in the world—the lust of the flesh, the lust of the eyes, and the pride of life—is not of the Father but is of the world."* Lust. Greed.

Pride. Does that not describe our world today? It also describes the world in which we were raised and the generations upon generations that came before us. The only difference between our generation and the generation we are raising is our children's early exposure to temptation.

Every person has basic needs for food, water, clothes, and shelter. But these things only provide for the physical needs we face. What about the needs of our soul and spirit? The need for love, respect, purpose, belonging? This generation is crying out for relationship, fellowship, and communication. (That's why there is such an addiction to social media.) They crave fame—the desire to be known. But the root of these desires can only be fulfilled in and through God.

Independent of Him, our eyes are never satisfied. Our ears will not quit itching. God created every person with a void in their heart that only He can fill. Knowledge will not fill that void. Stuff will not fill the void. As parents, our job is to know God's love for ourselves so we can love our children and introduce them to God's kind of love. Our kids will be okay without those $400 pair of athletic shoes. They won't be okay without love—real love—the kind that comes from God (1 John 4:10).

Everyone's greatest need is to know the love of God. To know they are accepted in the beloved (Ephesians 1:6). To know God's purpose for their life. These things are common to us all. And as Christian parents we can help our children discover them before they leave our home, through both our model and the way we structure their lives.

God's kind of love is different from the "love" of this world. The world's version of love is selfish and sensual. It doesn't give unconditionally. It takes. God's love is a gift. It isn't earned or deserved (Romans 5:8). Neither does it fade with time or performance

(Jeremiah 31:3). But it does have to be taught. If the only kind of love our children encounter is the selfish, conditional love of the world, they will think God loves the same way. Our children need to be able to discern the difference between God's agape love and the counterfeit love the world offers. The best way I know to do that is with the love checklist from 1 Corinthians 13.

Love suffers long and is kind; love does not envy; love does not parade itself, is not puffed up; does not behave rudely, does not seek its own, is not provoked, thinks no evil; does not rejoice in iniquity, but rejoices in the truth; bears all things, believes all things, hopes all things, endures all things. Love never fails...
(1 Corinthians 13:4-8).

Other kinds of love do exist (love for friends, sexual love, family love, self-love, etc.), but none are sustainable by themselves. They are too easily perverted. The 16 character traits of love from 1 Corinthians describe the way God loves us, and the way we ought to love each other. Let's look at each one.

1. **Love suffers long**. It never gives up. It is patient and enduring. It sees and expresses God's goodness over the long haul.
2. **Love is kind**. It is not just friendly or full of warm, fuzzy feelings. Love cares more for others than for self. It seeks the good of others.
3. **Love does not envy**. It does not want what it does not have. It is content and thankful.
4. **Love does not parade itself**. It is not boastful. It doesn't require the limelight or try to draw attention to itself. It is willing to share the stage.

5. **Love is not puffed up**. It is not prideful and arrogant. It doesn't think more highly of self than it should.
6. **Love does not behave rudely.** The Message Bible says love does not *"force itself on others."* No one who says, "If you love me, you will…" is acting in love. True love does not force itself on anyone. It is not rude.
7. **Love does not seek its own.** It is not demanding or selfish. It does not insist on its own rights. It isn't self-centered.
8. **Love is not easily provoked**. It isn't touchy or resentful. It does not fly off the handle in anger.
9. **Love thinks no evil.** Love doesn't keep record of wrong. It doesn't hold people's past over them or dream up ways of getting even. Love forgives.
10. **Love does not rejoice in iniquity**. It doesn't reveal when others fail. It doesn't celebrate evil or condone what God condemns. It takes no pleasure in injustice or unrighteousness.
11. **Love rejoices in the truth**. It takes pleasure in truth. It follows truth and rejoices when truth is made known.
12. **Love bears all things**. It never gives up, gives in, or gives out regardless of circumstance. When it can't see a way out, love keeps going. When it has been hurt beyond measure, love chooses to keep loving.
13. **Love believes all things**. It keeps trusting God. It believes that God's Word is true, and that He is faithful to perform His Word. Love knows it is not our job to change people. It's our job to be consistent; to love them and share the truth believing that God will change them.
14. **Love hopes all things**. The Message Bible says it always looks for the best. It doesn't ignore the bad but strives to find the good in every circumstance. No matter what someone

has done or how they have failed, if they know Jesus, there is still good. And if they don't know Jesus but are still breathing, there is still time. Don't give up hope.

15. **Love endures all things**. It never looks back or considers quitting. Love keeps going until the end.
16. **Love never fails**. It never dies. You may kill other kinds of love, but God's love always rises from the dead. It does not change or wear out. It can be trusted.

This is the way God loves us. And because His love resides in us, this is how we ought to love each other. Teaching this to your children will not only protect them from counterfeit loves but will help them love their own families when they leave your home.

LOVE OVER FEAR

As parents, we don't have to fear the world's influence on our children. We don't have to fear circumstances or Satan's attacks. And we don't have to fear failure. Receiving God's love for us and teaching it to our children casts out fear. Even if we fall, we do not have to fear God's judgment or rejection. God will chasten and correct us, but never out of wrath. He loves us.

While there will always be natural consequences connected to sin, for both the saved and the lost, God does not punish us for our failings. He promised to never leave us or forsake us. God loves us just as we are—unconditionally—with the full intent, by His grace, to make us what He ordained us to be. First John says:

> *Whosoever shall confess that Jesus is the Son of God, God dwelleth in him and he in God. And we have known and believed the love that God hath to us.* **God is love***; and he that dwelleth in love, dwelleth in God, and God in him. Herein is our love made perfect, that we may have boldness in the day of judgment: because as he is, so are we in this world. There is no fear in love;* **but perfect love casteth out fear** *because fear hath torment. He that feareth is not made perfect in love* (1 John 4:15-18 KJV).

Every generation deals with four basic fears: the fear of faces (humans), the fear of fences (obstacles), the fear of failure, and the fear of foes.

Fear of Faces

As believers who understand God's love, we should not fear people. The Bible says, *"The fear of man brings a snare"* (Proverbs 29:25). It's a trap. Just look at the strange things people do to fit in. The fear of rejection is powerful in all our lives, but with the rise of social media it is being amplified among our young people. Today, children not only fear the rejection of their peers, but they also fear the rejection of people they've never even met. Only the love of God can cast out that fear.

As parents, we need to help our children deal with this fear early so it doesn't follow them into adulthood. And follow it will. No one outgrows the fear of rejection. Just think about the political peer pressure we've seen in the last decade; the peer pressure to silence conviction in the workplace or give in to instant gratification. The fear of what others think of us does not disappear as we age. It is overcome through our knowledge of God's love.

The fear of faces is a twofold problem with two simple solutions—the fear of rejection (which disappears when we realize we are already accepted by the Creator of the universe according to Ephesians 1:6) and the need for affirmation. In John chapter 12 certain Jews who believed in Jesus refused to confess Him as Lord *"...lest they should be put out of synagogue, for they loved the praise of men more than the praise of God"* (John 12:42-43). Did you know God praises you? Zephaniah says God rejoices over you with singing (Zephaniah 3:17). The NLT version of that verse reads, *"With His love He will calm all your fears. He will rejoice over you with joyful songs."* Isn't that amazing?! When Christians don't believe this, they crave the praises of people instead.

Only in knowing God's acceptance and affirmation are we able to handle the fear of man. Rejection hurts. It doesn't matter if you're a child or an adult. But when we know we are accepted by God as the Father to His child and that God is pleased with our faith (Hebrews 11:6), what can anyone do to us (Romans 8:31)?

FEAR OF FENCES

Everyone faces obstacles or challenges in life that have to be overcome by faith. But isn't that how we are called to live—by faith (2 Corinthians 5:7)? Faith moves mountains. Our children need to learn to live by and operate in faith so they can speak to whatever mountains they encounter in life (Mark 11:23).

"What does faith have to do with love?" I hear you asking. Well, Galatians 5:6 says that *"in Christ Jesus neither circumcision nor uncircumcision counts for anything, but only faith working through love."* Our faith only works when we understand God's love. When we know God loves us, no matter what happens or what obstacle we face, we know we never walk alone (Hebrews 13:5). We will overcome (Revelation 12:11; Romans 8:37). *"God is our refuge and strength, an ever-present help in trouble"* (Psalm 46:1 NIV).

Fear of Failure

My generation dealt with a fear of failure and a desire for success unlike any other before it. Look at all the self-help books that flooded the market during that time; the number of people who became millionaires before they turned 40. Even most of the preaching in that era was about how to be a success. But this generation is dealing with fear on steroids. This generation fears insignificance. They have an unhealthy desire for fame and recognition. If they don't have their own YouTube channel or a viral post on TikTok by the time they're 16, they feel like a failure. The number of followers they have on social media has become their standard of success. That's why being defriended or blocked is such a big deal. Our children are not content with four or five face-to-face friends; they want the entire world to know who they are. They are driven by a fear of failure in the sense of their need for significance. Only the love of God can cast out that fear in their hearts.

Though they may not realize it yet, your child's greatest need is to be known and loved by God. When our identity is wrapped up in Christ, and we have been crucified to the world and its desires (including our number of followers), we are not controlled by those fears and it's easier to believe. It's easier to trust. How can we fear failure when we're already a success in Christ, when we're already known in heaven? Do we want to have an impact in this world? Yes. Do we want to make a difference? Of course. But we can't be driven by unhealthy fears.

FEAR OF FOES

Our kids also need to know that Satan is real, and his opposition can be fierce (1 Corinthians 16:9). We can't avoid or ignore the demonic forces arrayed against God's will for our lives. But neither should we fear them. Jesus stripped our adversary of power at the Cross (Colossians 2:15). Now, we can overcome any spiritual battle we face by faith. That does not mean we won't face persecution. We will, and our children need to be prepared for that. But they also need to know they are equipped to win!

> *Finally, my brethren, be strong in the Lord and in the power of His might. Put on the whole armor of God, that you may be able to stand against the wiles of the devil. For we do not wrestle against flesh and blood, but against principalities, against powers, against the rulers of the darkness of this age, against spiritual hosts of wickedness in the heavenly places. Therefore take up the whole armor of God, that you may be able to withstand in the evil day, and having done all, to stand. Stand therefore, having girded your waist with truth, having put on the breastplate of righteousness, and having shod your feet with the preparation of the gospel of peace; above all, taking the shield of faith with which you will be able to quench all the fiery darts of the wicked one. And take the helmet of salvation, and the sword of the Spirit, which is the word of God; praying always with all prayer and supplication in the Spirit, being watchful to this end with all perseverance and supplication for all the saints* (Ephesians 6:10-18).

A spiritual battle can only be won with spiritual weapons, so ensure your children have the six pieces of armor outlined in

Ephesians chapter 6. Teach them that these weapons are theirs by faith in Jesus (Ephesians 1:3). But putting them on does not equip them for battle; putting them on *is* the battle.

- *Girdle (or belt) of Truth:* Our children need to know the power of truth. We need to teach them that all lies come from Satan, the father of lies, and we defeat him by embracing Truth.
- *Breastplate of Righteousness:* We have been made righteous by faith in Jesus. And this righteousness of the heart trumps self-righteousness. It protects us from Satan's weapons of guilt and condemnation.
- *Gospel Shoes of Peace:* The gospel of peace prepares us to walk into the world with confidence. We know that God loves us. He has forgiven us and made peace with us through the blood of His Cross. And since we are at peace with God, we can overcome Satan's schemes of division and walk in peace with others.
- *Shield of Faith:* The shield of faith quenches all the fiery darts of Satan. It reminds us that we can't be overcome by evil when we've already been made an overcomer in Christ (1 John 5:4-5).
- *Helmet of Salvation:* The battlefield of the spirit is the mind. Every time we embrace God's thoughts (His Word) over the world's, we win. Teach your children the joy and power of their salvation, and watch Satan lose his hold on them.
- *Sword of the Spirit:* The sword of the Spirit is the Word of God. Read His Word. Speak His Word. It will be like a sword piercing the enemy. It will change things in the spirit, which, in turn, changes what we see in the natural.

10

ROD OF CORRECTION

The rod and reproof give wisdom: but a child left to himself bringeth his mother to shame.

—*Proverbs 29:15 KJV*

When children are very young, part of their training involves the "rod of reproof" (Proverbs 29:15). The rod (also known as spanking) is a temporary form of discipline used in the early childhood stage when children need a physical, concrete example that obedience brings life and blessing, and disobedience causes pain. In my experience, this mode of discipline is most effective between the ages of two to approximately ten. With my own children, it lasted until they were about eight.

Let me be very clear. The "rod of reproof or correction" is not a rod of wrath. Once a child can reason and understand boundaries, consequences, and the principle of sowing and reaping, other forms of discipline and chastening are just as effective. In fact, for most older children, when the consequence of their disobedience involves grounding or the loss of privileges (such as fasting social media), they would rather receive a spanking. In their mind, the spanking is less painful. It is quick and simple, whereas other forms of discipline can be extended for days. Regardless of the form of correction used, children should never be disciplined out of anger or frustration. All forms of discipline must stem from love. *"The wrath of man worketh not the righteousness of God"* (James 1:20).

The purpose of correction—the rod and reproof or instruction—is wisdom. A child who does not understand why they are being disciplined will not grow in wisdom. It is up to parents to communicate, at an appropriate age level, both what the child did wrong (disobeyed or did not honor) and how to make it right. Offering only the rod (the physical consequence) is not enough. Likewise, only reproving (lecturing) young children will not produce results. Children need both the rod *and* reproof.

Proverbs 13:24 tells us, *"He who spares his rod **hates** his son, but he who **loves** him disciplines him promptly."* Withholding discipline from our children is a form of hate. They grow up unable to function in careers, marriage, or society. They have no sense of boundaries, consequences, or personal responsibility, which leads to a life of self-destruction. Discipline, then, is a form of love. Most people think of love and hate as emotions rather than actions or inactions. But 1 John 3:18 says, *"My little children, let us not love in word or in tongue, but in **deed** and in **truth**."* Love is an action; it corrects when necessary. Hate is an inaction; it ignores wrongs to keep *self* comfortable. According to scripture, parents who do not discipline their children hate them.

Why the Rod?

I think we all understand that misusing the rod (using it in anger, wielding it too hard or for too long, using it at too young or old of an age) is not healthy. But what is the purpose of the rod? The rod demonstrates the existence and purpose of boundaries. It uproots foolishness and provides consequences that are easily understood at every level. When used properly, the rod proves our love to our children and helps them learn to discern and resist temptation. The rod is a temporary form of discipline that protects parents from verbally abusing their children or cursing them with angry words. It gives children a concrete example of the pain self-centeredness brings, and it shows them the power of sowing and reaping.

To be successful, children must learn early that life is governed by rules and boundaries. Everywhere they go, in every season, there will be rules. Refusing to submit to godly boundaries hurts ourselves and others. And not correcting our children when they overstep those boundaries hardens their heart to sin. Without the intervention of God's mercy and grace, that hardness will ultimately lead to their rejection of Christ. But learning to recognize and live within godly boundaries leads to blessing. It protects us from harm.

Proverbs 22:15 says, *"Foolishness is bound up in the heart of a child: the rod of correction will drive it far from him."* Notice again it is the "rod of correction," not the rod of wrath or anger. Many believe the rod was an instrument of Old Covenant wrath. They think it damages people. While the rod can harm others when used in wrath, so can verbal abuse, guilt, condemnation, and hollering. Without the rod, scripture says, foolishness remains bound in our children's hearts.

Dear one, we are not wiser than God. We must understand that not dealing with foolishness in our children's lives will harm them forever. The rod was never part of the law. It was revealed in Proverbs, the book of wisdom. Under the law, rebellious children were stoned to death (Mark 7:10; Exodus 21:17; Leviticus 20:9). Spanking offers them mercy! The rod of correction then is not connected to the curses of the law; it is connected to the blessings of wisdom. The rod gives our children consequences when the results of sowing and reaping are too far removed for a little one's understanding.

Young children need immediate consequences. They can't reason cause and effect, sowing and reaping, action and reaction. The rod is how children learn personal responsibility. It's a form of hate not to teach our children that there are consequences to their actions. An entire generation has been raised to believe their problems are someone else's fault, and now their lives are being destroyed because they won't take responsibility for their mistakes and poor life choices.

The rod trains children early so that foolishness and disobedience causes pain. In our home, the rod was called "Mr. Spoon." None of our children wanted to experience Mr. Spoon on their hind ends, but it taught them early the value of obedience and the consequence of disobedience. Many parents avoid the rod because they don't believe in hurting children. I don't believe in hurting children either, but the Bible is clear: *"Do not withhold correction from a child, for if you beat him with a rod, he will not die. You shall beat him with a rod and deliver his soul from hell"* (Proverbs 23:13-14). The purpose of the rod is correction, not punishment. Not harm, wrath, or a release of parental anger. God's Word never implies we are to hurt our children. Instead, this temporary form of discipline serves to save them from the eternal consequence of sin.

In all discipline, parents must keep the end goal in mind. We are preparing our children for adulthood. An undisciplined child is unemployable—and that will hurt them. An undisciplined child is likely to wind up in divorce—and that will hurt both them and their families. An undisciplined child may go to prison—and that will hurt their future. But I can think of no greater hurt than a child who has no concept of personal accountability going to hell. That kind of hurt truly harms them. It lasts for eternity.

Young children have no concept of temptation. They don't know they are being selfish, nor do they understand the harm that causes. They can't discern Satan's devises. Thus, a parent should not expect a three-year-old to resist the temptation to take their brother's toy when all the parent has done is warn them of the dangers of selfishness. They can't think in abstract concepts like that. They don't consider long-term effects. Their brains are not yet developed enough to understand, "If you continue operating in self-centeredness and pride, you won't have any friends in school. You won't be able to hold down a job. You won't be able to function in marriage and family; you'll probably end up in divorce, paying alimony for the rest of your life.

"To cope, you'll abuse drugs and alcohol, become homeless, and resort to dumpster-diving for food. You could even end up in prison where someone will steal all of your stuff just like you stole your brother's toy. That will teach you for being selfish!" Children can't understand any of that. What they can understand is, "If you take your brother's toy again, we will have a meeting with Mr. Spoon."

I've said it before, but it bears repeating: The rod of correction gives children a concrete example of the pain self-centeredness brings. Self-centeredness is pride. Pride leads to strife, conflict, failure, and destruction (Proverbs 13:10, 16:18). *"Only by pride cometh contention: but with the well advised is wisdom"* (Proverbs 13:10 KJV). Be "well-advised." Understand that any disobedience in your child is a result of pride in their heart. And according to God's wisdom, the rod will put a restraint on that selfishness and teach them to prefer others. It is an external form of denying self; one that, if learned early, will help them resist the destructive temptations of drugs, alcohol, and digital media.

I like to conduct the Walmart test to gauge where my children are on the "learning to deny self" scale. (The Walmart test is a rite of passage for every child and parent. But it doesn't have to happen at Walmart. Any store will do.) When your child wants something you were not already planning to buy, it is good to say, "Not now." This test helps them learn to harness their emotions and develop patience. And it teaches you the same thing—especially if they have a walleyed fit, fall on the floor and start foaming at the mouth while doing a 360. Just remember, this denying of self is a development process for both of you.

You see, the proper use of the rod teaches children, in a concrete way, to deny self and resist the devil. Then, as adults, they will be able to understand James 4:7 which says, *"Therefore submit to God. Resist the devil and he will flee from you."* The rod teaches children that pride and self-centeredness cause strife and contention and will eventually lead to destruction (Proverbs 11:2, 13:10, 16:18).

It's Only Temporary

When we talk about the rod, we are talking about a short-term, time-tested form of discipline in which a flat-sided object (not the hand) strikes a child's gluteus maximus with precise precision. This "spanking" sends a signal to your child's brain that opens tear ducts and engages the synapsis that fire a message to the child that says, "I'm not doing that again." We're not talking about beating a child in anger or wrath. A spanking is one to two swats delivered to their bottoms followed by instruction, hugs, and prayer.

"Well, doesn't that defeat the purpose?" you ask.

Absolutely not. The purpose of a spanking isn't to guilt the child or punish them with your disapproval. Its purpose is to train them in boundaries. A spanking is a consequence for disobedience; then we move on, providing our children with a biblical pattern of repentance and restoration. We hug them to show them we are not angry, nor are we going to hold anything over them. Instead, we love them enough to bring correction and train them in the way they should go.

We pray together as a way to show our kids that God is also involved in this process of growth and that He is faithful and just to forgive us and cleanse us from all unrighteousness (1 John 1:9).

Scripture is clear. God disciplines those He loves (Hebrews 12:6). He chastens and corrects all His legitimate children, but He does not do so in anger. While *"no chastening seems to be joyful for the present, but painful; nevertheless, afterward it yields the peaceable fruit of righteousness to those who have been trained by it"* (Hebrews 12:11). If God does this for us, why would we not discipline our children? Do we not want them to experience the *"peaceable fruit of righteousness"*? Do we not want to prepare them for the chastening of the Lord? The time they are with us—the time our children experience the physical rod of correction—is temporary. But it will yield great rewards!

Much of our lives rotate around the principle of sowing and reaping. *"Do not be deceived, God is not mocked; for whatsoever a man sows, that will he also reap. For he who sows to his flesh will of his flesh reap corruption, but he who sows to the Spirit will of the Spirit reap everlasting life"* (Galatians 6:7-8). When we sow to our flesh in thought or action, we reap corruption. Not from God, but from our flesh. Corruption is the process by which something goes from good to bad. We can all corrupt the good God wills for our lives by sowing bad seeds. But children can't comprehend that. It is too abstract or abstruse. So the rod teaches them, on a small scale, how sowing and reaping works. "If I disobey, I will reap Mr. Spoon. So, I think I will choose to obey. Then I will reap a reward (even if that reward is simply the absence of pain)."

Unfortunately, many parents are deceived over the reality of sowing and reaping. They don't realize the harvest they are experiencing, even as it relates to their children's behavior, is a result of the seeds they have sown. Someone or something else is always to blame. Regardless, God is not mocked. His Word is true. Avoiding this principle and rejecting God's wisdom will only lead to corruption. *"There is a way that seems right to a man, but its end is the way of death"* (Proverbs 14:12).

While it is true that we reap some things in life we didn't sow to, most of the time, the pain in our lives is a direct result of the seeds we have sown. But thank God for His mercy! We can repent and experience crop failure on those bad seeds, and we can sow good seeds, believing for the harvest of righteousness in our lives. So discipline your children, for their sakes, and for the sake of our future. Consider God's wisdom and raise functional, disciplined children who will grow into fruitful, blessed adults.

I know I have said this over and over, but it is the rod of *correction* parents wield, not the rod of anger (Proverbs 22:15). Too many parents don't understand the purpose of the rod, or they fear using it and harming their children. Yet they yell and threaten and cuss their kids. They get frustrated and call them names or slap them. These things are not okay. They are a result of human anger and will not produce the righteousness of God

(James 1:20). Only loving discipline can drive foolishness out of a child's heart.

Parents who reject the rod, calling it abusive, yet curse their children with harsh words are verbally abusing them. And those words can last a lifetime. Parents say things such as, "You never do anything right," or, "You'll never amount to anything." They call their child names and rewrite their identity when they say, "You're such a headache," or, "You're nothing but a pain in my [you can fill in the blank]." These kinds of word curses cause great damage to a child's development. Parents who withhold correction and loving discipline from their children are not thinking of the eternal consequences of disobedience and rebellion (Proverbs 23:13-14). And parents who discipline their children in anger are not modeling the loving correction of our heavenly Father.

Colossians 4:6 says, *"Let your speech always be with grace, seasoned with salt...."* We are all called to be kind and forgiving to one another. That includes our children.

> *Let no corrupt word proceed out of your mouth, but what is good for necessary edification, that it may impart grace to the hearers. And do not grieve the Holy Spirit.... Let all bitterness, wrath, anger, clamor, and evil speaking be put away from you.... And be kind to one another, tenderhearted, forgiving one another, even as God in Christ forgave you* (Ephesians 4:29-32).

We need to bless our children with our words and actions, even in discipline.

11

Provoke Not to Wrath

> *And you, fathers, do not provoke your children to wrath, but bring them up in the training and admonition of the Lord.*
> —Ephesians 6:4

As with all things in life, parenthood requires balance. As parents, we are instructed to train our children (from birth to 10) and admonish or teach them (from 10 to 20) in the Lord. But in that training and teaching, we are also commanded not to provoke our children to wrath. Often, well-meaning parents mishandle discipline situations with their children in a desire for them to be and do all God has for them. If we are not careful to repent of those missteps, we can provoke our children to wrath. (*Provoke* means to anger, enrage, exasperate, or vex someone.) The most common things that provoke or exasperate children are anger and impatience, inconsistency, neglect, abuse, unclear expectations or consequences, humiliation, favoritism, harshness, and unreasonable punishments. Let's look more intently at each of these missteps.

Anger and Impatience

Like reproduces like; so we must be careful how we approach our children. Anger and impatience from us will not bring out the best in them. *"...let every man be swift to hear, slow to speak, slow to wrath; for the wrath of man does not produce the righteousness of God"* (James 1:19-20). Often, parents feel that no one listens unless they raise their voices or show anger. But the end never justifies the means. Scripture admonishes us to be quick to listen, slow to speak, and very slow to become angry. As parents, we are our children's role models. Our discipline is preparing them for relationship with the heavenly Father, so our chastening needs to model His.

Remember, at 20, they will come out from under our covering and instruction and come under His. It is our job to prepare them for the way God disciplines and chastens. He never disciplines in wrath, impatience, condemnation, or guilt. I love the way The Passion Translation relays this verse: *"Be quick to listen, but slow to speak. And be slow to become angry, for human anger is never a legitimate tool to promote God's righteous purpose."* Anger from you will reproduce anger in your child. Remember, godly discipline is about them and their future, not your feelings. When angry, we create bias and become unqualified to discipline; so, if emotions become heightened, in any form of discipline, call for a timeout. Recuse yourself and pray before moving forward. You don't want to do or say something that will misrepresent God to your child. You may be the one who needs the time-out chair.

INCONSISTENCY

When we discipline emotionally, we are inconsistent. If our children are only disciplined when we've had a bad day, and at all other times their bad behavior is ignored, we breed feelings of confusion and insecurity. Insecurity leads to fear, and fear destroys faith. Disobedience can't be wrong today but okay tomorrow, depending on our mood. Children need consistency. Without it, they will create consistency for themselves—even if that "consistency" is in the form of pushing your buttons until you erupt in anger.

Neglect

Scripture says, *"a child left to himself brings shame to his mother"* (Proverbs 29:15). We see the reality of this play out in culture every day. Children need boundaries. They need discipline in order to become productive and fruitful. Without it, they become hurt and angry. They feel abandoned and struggle to trust. These symptoms are especially prevalent in the adolescent stage. Parents, don't let your teenage children con you into believing they don't want you in their lives. They want and need your attention at 15 just as much as they did at 5. When they don't receive it in loving affirmation, they will demand it by acting out. So when your children or grandchild cry, "Watch this Papaw!" take the time to affirm your love and give them your attention.

Abuse

Second Corinthians 10:8 tells us that all authority comes from God for the purpose of edification, not destruction. As parents, we cannot be abusive with any form of discipline. I once sent one of my children to their room with, "Don't come out until you draw your first social security check." Too far? Of course! But we all laughed, and my method lost any similitude of discipline. Proverbs 28:15-16 says, *"Like a roaring lion and a charging bear is a wicked ruler over poor people. A ruler who lacks understanding is a great oppressor...."* We need understanding and self-awareness to be good parents, otherwise we end up oppressing our children instead of being their coaches and instructors in life.

In all things, physical and verbal abuse is unacceptable for the Christian. Proverbs 18:21 says, *"Death and life are in the power of the tongue, and those who love it will eat its fruit."* Our words matter, so choose them wisely. Even in discipline, be gracious (Colossians 4:6). Don't put your children down or shut them down with wrong words. And if you do, apologize quickly.

UNCLEAR EXPECTATIONS AND CONSEQUENCES

It is not right or fair to discipline a child for something they don't know is wrong. If you have not given clear instructions, how can a child be held accountable to them? In all expectations, check for understanding. Did your child hear the rule or boundary given? Do they understand the consequences of disobedience? Without clarity in these things, we can provoke our children to wrath. For example, with adolescents: "Your curfew is at 10 p.m. What are the consequences if you're late? If you're late and these consequences are invoked, who's fault is that?" At this stage, we are not looking for blind obedience. We are teaching our children to process their actions, count the cost, and own their mistakes. Critical thinking is part of preparing them for adulthood.

HUMILIATION

The goal of discipline is never to shame or embarrass our children, even if they embarrass us by throwing a fit at Walmart. That is just a parental rite of passage. It can be brutal, but don't give in to the temptation to cast the demon out of your child in the aisle or at the checkout line. Breathe. Count to ten, then deal with it in private. Don't humiliate your child. Be the adult. First Peter and Proverbs both say, *"Love covers the multitude of sin"* (1 Peter 4:8, Proverbs 10:12). That doesn't mean love excuses sin or tries to cover it up. But, like God, love doesn't expose or damage people publicly. First Corinthians 13:5 says love *"does not behave rudely, does not seek its own, is not provoked, thinks no evil."* And Romans 13:10 (KJV) says, *"Love worketh no ill to his neighbour; therefore love is the fulfilling of the law."* We represent God most fully when we love with His kind of love and do not work ill toward others.

Favoritism

God does not show favoritism, and neither should we. While I have been accused of having favorites, I am innocent. I can't help that my youngest daughter is nearly perfect! Even my oldest son agrees. She is his favorite, too. She really is special to us all, but favoritism can be a problem especially among blended families. Favoritism provokes children to wrath. Remember the story of Joseph and his brothers in Genesis 37? Jacob's favoritism toward Joseph was not wise. It provoked jealousy among the brothers, and they eventually conspired to sell Joseph into slavery.

> But when his brothers saw that their father loved [Joseph] more than all his brothers, they hated him and could not say, Peace [in friendly greeting] to him or speak peaceably to him (Genesis 37:4 AMPC).

While there is no excuse for what the brothers did, Jacob didn't help. In all families, favoritism needs to be watched for and dealt with quickly. This requires self-awareness on the part of the parents, and possibly some hard conversations between the two. There may be a blind spot in one of you that needs a second pair of eyes.

Harshness

Being too hard or too strict with our children can discourage them. Many times, when we recognize a weakness of the flesh or respond to a child's failure, we react harshly. We forget that we are not only correcting and instructing them in righteousness, but also demonstrating God's grace and mercy to them. We must be gracious to our children in their mistakes so that we teach them to run *to* God, not *from* Him in their shortcomings. Be quick to forgive your children and extend mercy whenever possible. Doing so expresses grace (getting the good we don't deserve) and mercy (not getting the bad we do deserve) in ways they will never forget.

Unreasonable Punishment

To keep from exasperating our kids in punishment, the time must match the crime. Just like we don't invoke capital punishment as a society for shoplifting, so we as parents don't ground our teenagers for six months the first time they miss curfew. As children get older, we transition away from the physical rod and begin to create (and discuss) consequences that are just and fair. At times, every teen thinks *any* amount of discipline is unreasonable, but this too is a learning experience. Equity is one of the seven pillars in the house of wisdom, so we must learn to mete out just and fair consequences without prejudice or partiality.

12

BLESSING OUR CHILDREN

The blessing of the Lord, it maketh rich, and he addeth no sorrow with it.

—*Proverbs 10:22 KJV*

In addition to correcting and discipling our children, we need to learn to bless them as the Lord blesses us. The blessing of the Lord makes us rich. But notice that riches aren't the blessing. The blessing is an intangible that affects the tangible realm. For example, people sometimes die and leave an abundance to their children, which is a good thing, unless they never taught their children how to handle wealth. That will lead to sorrow. It could even destroy them. God's blessing is not like that. With God's blessing riches flow without sorrow.

The blessing of God is grace or favor. It is God's acceptance, affirmation, and good pleasure toward us (Ephesians 1:3-6). All of us need that affirmation, and we need to learn to give it to our children. When Jesus received the blessing of His Father at baptism, *"This is My beloved Son, in whom I am well pleased"* (Matthew 3:17), it jumpstarted His ministry. Affirmation from a father is powerful. Your children need to know you are pleased with them.

God's promises are also His blessings. When God blessed Abraham in Genesis 12, He did so by making a promise based on His character, not Abraham's conduct. This allowed God to perform the promise on Abraham's behalf (Romans 4:20). In Christ, God fulfills all His promises this way (2 Corinthians 1:20). All we have to do is believe (Galatians 3:13-15). What a blessing!

In ancient times, the blessing was viewed as something finite. It could only be given to one person in the family—typically, the heir, the eldest son. In Genesis 12, God blessed Abraham, who in turn, blessed his son Isaac. Though not Abraham's firstborn, Isaac was the promised seed. He was the child of faith. Without the fulfillment of God's promise, Abraham and Sarah could not get pregnant. Sarah suggested Abraham use her handmaid to beget children. Abraham agreed and sired Ishmael. Ishmael was born of the flesh, the work of man, and we are still dealing with those consequences today. Eventually, Abraham returned to faith in God's promise of a son by Sarah, and Isaac was born. Isaac carried the faith of Abraham in his heart, so Abraham gave him the blessing.

Isaac had two sons: the twins, Jacob and Esau. Esau, who was born first, had no desire for the things of God. He sold his birthright for a bowl of soup. Later, as Isaac lay dying, Jacob and his mother, Rebekah, deceived Isaac into giving the blessing of the firstborn to him instead of Esau (Genesis 27:21-29). When Esau heard his father had given Jacob the blessing *"he cried with an exceedingly great and bitter cry, and said to his father, 'Bless me—me also, O my father!'"* (Genesis 27:34). Jacob, on the other hand, learned a great lesson and did something different with his blessing. As a man of faith, he passed the blessing on to all twelve of his sons! God used that blessing to charter a nation and make Jacob's sons into the twelve tribes of Israel.

Like Esau, I believe that today, young and old alike are crying out for their father's blessing. When that blessing is withheld, especially in youth, it breaks the spirit of a child and causes great sorrow. Those children grow up still craving their father's blessing or approval. They seek approval from others and are unable to properly relate to a loving heavenly Father. Let us not do that to our children.

Speak a Blessing

Blessings are given through words. In the book of Numbers, God told Moses to explain this concept to Aaron so he could bless Israel.

> *This is the way you shall bless the children of Israel. Say to them: "The Lord bless you and keep you; the Lord make His face shine upon you, and be gracious to you; the Lord lift up His countenance upon you, and give you peace." So they shall put My name on the children of Israel, and I will bless them* (Numbers 6:22-27).

God speaks blessings over us, and we must speak blessings—words of love, favor, honor, and God's promises—over our children so that He can bless them.

What we say and pray over our children matters. Proverbs 18:21 says, *"Death and life are in the power of the tongue: and those who love it shall eat its fruit."* Words bless and words curse; they bring life or death. Let's speak life over our children and bless them.

The Blessing of Touch

The blessing of God is also given through touch, or the laying on of hands. (This is also how the anointing is transmitted.) When

Jesus received the little children in Mark 10:16, scripture says, *"He took them up in His arms, laid His hands on them, and blessed them."* At this same time, Jesus was correcting His disciples and telling them that to enter God's kingdom, we need the faith of a child.

This "laying on of hands" is how Moses blessed Joshua before he died (Numbers 27:18-23). It is how Jacob blessed his grandsons Ephraim and Manasseh (Genesis 48:9-20). It is also how Paul blessed a young pastor named Timothy. In 2 Timothy 1:6, Paul writes to Timothy, *"Therefore I remind you to stir up the gift of God which is in you through the laying on of my hands."* Paul was referring to the time Timothy was anointed and prophesied over in 1 Timothy chapter 4. As parents, we are in charge of laying hands on our children and speaking blessings over them. We can do this anytime, but an easy way to build this practice into your family routine is to pray over them at night. Lay hands on them in their beds and speak God's promises over them.

THE BLESSING OF FORGIVENESS

Perhaps the most profound blessing you can give your child is that of forgiveness. Apologizing recognizes the inherent value and dignity of others. Saying "I'm sorry, please forgive me," showcases how you value someone. It models humility and grants them respect. It is impossible to go through this life, your marriage, or parenthood without making a mistake. We all know that, but too often pride prevents us from verbalizing it. Yet scripture says humility is the number-one ingredient for a successful life. *"... Yes, all of you be submissive to one another, and be clothed with humility, for 'God resists the proud, but gives grace to the humble.' Therefore humble yourselves under the mighty hand of God, that He may exalt you in due time"* (1 Peter 5:5-6).

When we humble ourselves before others and reveal our need for mercy, we simultaneously reveal another's need to forgive. There is an underlying anger in the hearts and minds of this generation that concerns me. It is hidden; under the radar, but it occasionally boils over in assaults and school shootings. I believe we're actually getting to the point where we could see a revolution, an internal war, in this country. We need to teach our children to be quick to forgive. And we need to model how to do that for others.

Asking for forgiveness cuts off anger, resentment, and bitterness before it can defile a heart or a relationship. When we model and ask for forgiveness, we deliver those we've hurt from torment. I remember coming home one time and seeing my second son's pigsty of a room. I don't remember how old he was, but I know his mom had instructed him to clean up and he had not obeyed. I raised my voice. I don't remember what I said, but it was something like, "Obey your mother and get this room cleaned up! Do it NOW!" I scared him. I had never raised my voice before, and I shouldn't have then, but I'd had a bad day and there was no cat to kick. When I walked out of the room, Sue told me I needed to go back. I turned around and saw my son crying.

"What's wrong?" I asked. (I was clueless as to how I had devastated him. Though what I said was not wrong, my tone was loud and harsh.)

"Dad, I'm so sorry. I didn't mean to let you down. I'm sorry I disappointed you."

"Whoa," I said. "You are not a disappointment to me. I was wrong to raise my voice at you. I'm sorry. Please forgive me. By the grace of God, I'll never raise my voice at you again."

That moment changed his life. It kept Satan from using unforgiveness to destroy the Word of God in his heart (Matthew 18:34; 2 Corinthians 2:11).

Another time, when our oldest was about 6 years old, we were celebrating the holidays at Sue's parents' home. I disciplined him for something and did so harshly, so I had to apologize. We both wept over it, and you know, I hardly remember him ever disobeying me after that. He never rebelled or questioned me through his teenage years. It was miraculous. My harshness could have damaged him for the rest of his life. It could have created an estranged relationship between us, but repentance changed that trajectory.

We all need to be quick to forgive and quick to repent. It is an attribute of God's love. First Corinthians says:

> *Love suffers long and is kind; love does not envy; love does not parade itself, is not puffed up; does not behave rudely, does not seek its own, is not provoked, thinks no evil; does not rejoice in iniquity, but rejoices in the truth; bears all things, believes all things, hopes all things, endures all things. Love never fails...* (1 Corinthians 13:4-8).

God's love empowers us to forgive, it enables us to fess up when we mess up knowing that our mistake will not change God's acceptance of us as His children. And when we ask someone, especially a child or family member, to forgive us, we express that truth to them as well.

Teaching

Listen, my son, and be wise, and direct your heart in the way [of the Lord].
— *Proverbs 23:19 AMP*

13

Preparation Time

My people are destroyed for lack of knowledge....
—Hosea 4:6

The next phase of child development is the teaching or preparation phase. This phase often overlaps a bit with the training phase because children are so curious. They start asking questions early in life. It is important, as parents, to discern what level of information children are requesting in those early questions and use wisdom in answering them in age-appropriate ways. There will be time in the teaching phase to answer them more fully.

The teaching phase typically starts between the ages of 8 to 10 (depending on a child's maturity level and their capacity to process and apply information) and goes through the teenage years. During this phase we equip our children for success in adulthood, marriage, and the fulfilling of God's will for their lives. Hosea 4:6 tells us that, *"My people are destroyed for lack of knowledge."* But Proverbs 10:11 says, *"The mouth of the righteous is a well of life...."* Parents need to be that well of life for their children during adolescence and teach them the ways of the Lord. Without it, they will perish.

Adolescence is the time of life when children begin to seek their own understanding and form their own opinions. And we need to encourage our children to do this by thinking for themselves, dissecting their feelings, and asking questions. Asking questions is a normal part of a teenager's developmental process. It is not rebellious—even when they ask questions about faith. With guidance, these questions can plant the seeds of faith needed to grow into healthy, independent adults who know how to trust God in all things.

No one can forsake wickedness or unrighteous thoughts without first learning to discern which thoughts belong to them and which belongs to another (Isaiah 55:7). Asking questions is part of seeking truth and wisdom; it is the path to maturity. But after asking questions, we need to encourage our children to take those questions to God. *"'Come now and let us reason together' says the Lord. 'Though your sins are like scarlet, they shall be white as snow...'"* (Isaiah 1:18).

Children must learn to think on their own, to pray on their own and seek God on their own, instead of relying on us to spoon-feed them. If they learn to ask questions instead of questioning God, they will grow in faith. Asking questions is a wrestling for understanding that leads to a solid faith built on a personal relationship with God. Questioning God is a symptom of doubt and unbelief. It asks, "Did God really say...?" which leads to a faith crisis, a walking away from God.

I think a lot of parents understand that their children need knowledge during this time, but they often don't know what to teach them. There is so much to learn, it can feel overwhelming. Over the years, I have discovered that there are four primary areas of transition that our children experience while under our covering. And they need help to navigate each in a healthy way. During this time, kids experience tremendous changes in their minds and bodies. They become aware of sexuality, and they begin feeling the pressure of choosing a vocation. They also have to navigate family role changes and witness, firsthand, an example of what it means to follow a biblical pattern. Good communication is essential during this phase of parenting. As is empathy, patience, and forgiveness. Let's look at each of these areas in greater detail.

THEIR BODIES

Adolescence is an awkward time. Bodies and minds are growing and changing rapidly, but not at the same rate. Bodies change faster than minds during the teenage years, which creates a host of challenges, for both parents and kids. (Studies suggest our brains aren't fully developed until age 25, and after raising four children, I tend to agree.) Teens are more self-conscience during this time. They are extremely sensitive and a bit uncomfortable in situations that used to not bother them. Their likes and dislikes evolve, and they have a tendency to respond in extremes—either silent retreat or head-on attack. We may be tempted to think they are "brain dead" or that we are losing our minds, but, again, this is all a normal, natural part of development. As parents, we must be extremely aware and flexible during this season.

SEXUALITY AWARENESS

Sexuality is part of the human condition; a gift from God, and God's Word has a lot to say about it. Sex is pure and precious—within boundaries. But our sexually charged culture has perverted sex like never before. Young children are being exposed to concepts and situations they are not mature enough to process. They need a factual, age-appropriate, godly perspective on sex.

They need to know the dangers of sex outside God's boundaries and the pleasure it brings within those boundaries (Hebrews 13:4). As parents, we are called to be their main source of information. We cannot put our head in the sand and neglect this area of our children's education. There are too many 16-year-old sexperts providing children with misinformation, not to mention the propaganda coming out of Hollywood and the media. So, when do you talk to your kids about sex? There's no one right age. You must be discerning and follow the Spirit's lead. If your children aren't interested in sex, put it off for as long as you can.

Protect their moral innocence. Build relationship with them and set a precedent for godly communication so you can be your child's first source of information, not the last. (The first source holds the greatest authority.) This is a naturally curious phase of their lives, and sexuality is part of that curiosity. Just keep in mind that this phase is a discovery process. It is unlikely your children will ask you every question they'll have about sex at once. And it is unlikely they will be ready for every answer at once. So, stay engaged. Know what media they're ingesting. Know their choice of friends. Know where (and with whom) they are spending their time. Be the parent. Guide and redirect them as needed and be willing and able to share information as their maturity level demands.

Vocational Pressure

Kids begin feeling the pressure to choose a vocation in middle school. And while we do need to assist them in finding God's will for their life, the most important thing we can do is help them build the character and skills they'll need outside our home. We need to assure them that their diligence in school will pay off. We need to help them develop integrity and a good work ethic and teach them the disciplines that will create healthy boundaries for their life. Questions such as: "What am I going to do for a living? What career path is for me? What are my strengths and weaknesses? What are my gifts and talents, and how do I develop them? Where do I go to college, or do I even need college? Is vocational-technical training right for me? What about Bible school? Where do I fit in the world?" can be stressful. But our children should not have to traverse those waters alone. We need to be there for them offering love and security as they discover who they are and what God has designed them for.

FAMILY ROLE CHANGES

Outside of traumatic events, the adolescent stage is also the first time our children experience role changes within the family. During the first stage of parenting, everything we do with our children is hands-on. We're like helicopters, hovering over their every move. But when our children enter the adolescent teaching phase, we land the helicopter and give them a little more freedom. We are still available, but not in the same way we were in the earlier phase. The first stage of parenting is all about obedience. This second stage focuses more on honor. In it we are teaching them independence from people and dependance on God. In this season we explain the "ways of the Lord" and prepare them for life outside our home. This role adjustment can take time to navigate, so be patient. Know that you may have to fire up that helicopter a few times during this season, but the goal remains growth and relationship.

As I said, while we are training our children for independent living, we are also training them to remain dependent on God—to own their faith. Independent thinking is part of that process. I know this scares many parents, but the testing of a child's faith, while still under our authority and covering, is a good thing. Our faith will not carry them through adulthood. They must establish their own belief system to overcome the pressures of this life.

We want our children to evaluate, "Do I believe what I believe because this is what *Mom* and *Dad* believe? Or do I believe it because *I* believe?" This requires the wisdom of God and the leading of the Holy Spirit, so keep your heart soft and pliable to hear God's voice. Don't make everything a teaching moment, but be aware of those moments when they come. Don't be preachy but give your children a living example of how faith works. Have fun together. Build relationship. Laugh and play and be willing to let some things go. You'll circle back around that mountain and have another chance to address the issue with them in the years to come.

Remember Ephesians 6:1–3 says, *"Children, obey your parents in the Lord, for this is right. Honor your father and mother, which is the first commandment with promise, that it may be well with you, and you may live long on the earth."* During the teaching season we begin moving away from the mandate to "obey," which is action-focused, to the heart-issue of "honor." Honor is respect. And though we do see the results of honor through actions, honor is really an attitude.

Just keep in mind that honor and appreciation are not the same thing. Appreciation recognizes the full worth of something. Our children will not always appreciate us. They will not always recognize the full worth of what we do. But we are not in this for the awards. We parent on assignment from God, and as such, we may have to make unpopular decisions. Don't be moved by your child's lack of appreciation, but do teach them to honor your decisions and your position as their God-given authority. Look to God for your affirmation and love your children enough to correct them.

One of the areas we teach our children to have independence in is finances. Children need to learn how to handle their own money, as early as possible. Let your children earn money around the house or for good grades. Make finances available to teach them tithing, saving, and delayed gratification. Help them get an entry-level job as a teenager to introduce them to the responsibilities of the work force. All these things help teach our children stewardship (the wise handling of money) and help them learn to conquer covetousness (the desire for what others have). Stewardship involves natural things. Covetousness involves the heart. Teaching our children delayed gratification is a discipline of both the heart and flesh that will serve them well later in life.

We also need to teach our children emotional independence. As their bodies and minds change, self-awareness skills (and the lack thereof) become more important and apparent. During this time, attitudes surface. But instead of squashing those attitudes, as parents often want to do, we must help our children understand, control, and adjust them. As parents, we cannot allow ourselves to get emotional when addressing their big emotions. We must teach them, both in word and deed, that emotions are real, but unreliable. They do not always reflect truth.

Emotions make great servants, but poor masters. Our children need to know that we cannot allow emotions to take the lead in our decision-making process. As a parent, you need to model this principle as you give discipline. By postponing discipline when you are emotional, you teach your children the value of self-control. Dating is another area in which this skill is essential.

Recreational dating has harmed more people than anything else I can think of. In our culture, the practice of dating—going to the movies alone, being in a car alone, and staying out until midnight—produces no positive fruit. In these situations, emotions jump into the driver's seat and lead us down the wrong path. Teach your kids a better way. (I will spend an entire chapter on this topic later in the book; but in a nutshell, the only biblical reason to "date" is courtship with the end goal of marriage.)

Though, we are working toward independence in this stage, that independence is regulated independence. Wise parents will loosen their strings gradually during this season. They will treat their children as adults when their children act like adults. Adults take personal responsibility for their actions. They operate within boundaries, and when they mess it up, they own it. They fix it. As parents, we are under no obligation to treat our children as adults when they act like children.

In 1 Corinthians 13:11 (NLT) Paul says, *"When I was a child, I spoke and thought and reasoned as a child. But when I grew up, I put away childish things."* Childish understanding, thinking, and speaking must be put away for adult treatment to happen. Too many times, parents offer privileges to children they would never offer an adult. For example, when would it ever be okay for an adult to be alone in a car with someone of the opposite sex for hours at night? Avoiding that situation is not an instance of "Don't you trust me?" It's wisdom. The point is, freedom comes with responsibility. We should only grant our children "adult" privileges when they behave as adults demonstrating good attitudes, godly character, and good judgment.

In all our teaching, we have to be careful during this stage to avoid the demand for and image of perfection. None of us are perfect. We have to quit pretending our kids are special and incapable of sin or beyond temptation. And we have to stop pretending we get it right every time. Never justify your child's actions when they are guilty. Don't teach them that the right excuse will allow them to escape the consequences of their misbehavior. Hold them lovingly accountable. And if you mess up, fess up! Be an example of faith and repentance. Tell them, "I'm sorry. I misspoke" or "I mishandled that situation." Your model of repentance will help them when they have to repent. It will show them what Christian transformation really means.

14

BUILDING HEALTHY ESTEEM

For I say, through the grace given to me, to everyone who is among you, not to think of himself more highly than he ought to think; but to think soberly, as God has dealt to each one a measure of faith.

—*Romans 12:3*

There is a saying about childhood that is not necessarily true. "Children are resilient." The truth is, children are sensitive. They can be easily hurt. The same is true of teenagers. These years are tough. As parents, we need to be fully, lovingly, empathetically engaged. While our children do not need to be pampered and babied, they do need comforted. That is how they develop resilience. Our kids need to know we love them. They need to know they are important. We cannot say, "I love you" too often. Nor can we say, "I love you" and not back up that statement with our actions. Love is engaged, interactive, and attentive.

I remember a couple who were separated years ago. After about a month of living apart, the man wrote his wife a poem and mailed it to her. She enjoyed it so much, he decided to send her one every week. The wife enjoyed his engagement, so he wrote her a poem every day. Eventually, the woman married the mailman. The point is, you love who you spend time with, who you live life with. For our children's sake, we need to remember that nothing can replace our presence, especially as it pertains to building a healthy esteem.

The foundation of a healthy esteem starts with Christ. And there are at least four other basics that contribute to our children's sense of worth and esteem:

1. A sense of belonging (both through our natural family and the family of God)
2. A sense of worth or value
3. Self-respect
4. A sense of accomplishment or competence

Let's look at each one in more detail.

A Sense of Belonging

God did not create any of us to be alone. He created us for fellowship, for relationship. In Genesis 2:18, our perfect God looked at the perfect man He created to care for a perfect garden in a perfect world and said, *"It is not good that man should be alone; I will make him a helper comparable to him."* If it wasn't good for Adam to be alone in perfection, it's not good for us to be alone.

Our children were not created to sit in a room, alone, with a computer or a gaming console "connecting" them with the outside world. They need real, face-to-face relationships. When young people are alone all the time, it leads to depression and anxiety.

Psalm 68:6 says that God sets the lonely in families. Family gives children a sense of belonging, of being part of something larger than themselves. Family contributes to their identity and the development of a healthy esteem.

Scripture is clear that "family" starts with marriage, a marriage between a male and female (Mark 10:6-7). Family grows with children and extends to include grandparents, uncles, aunts, and cousins. One of the challenges of this generation is the consequence of the breakup and scattering of the family unit. My own children only saw their paternal grandparents a few times in their life. In previous generations, families rarely separated by more than 30 miles. Children grew up in areas where they were related to nearly half the town, and there was good in that. (That's why throughout much of the US, towns are only about 15 to 30 miles apart. That was as far as you could travel by horse in one day.)

People had a sense of belonging then. They knew who they were. Today, extended families are spread worldwide. More than half of American families have experienced divorce or never been married at all. Some divorcees create blended families, which is a good thing when done right with God's intervention. But my point is, the family unit has suffered, and our children are suffering as a result.

Thank God for the family of God!

The Church saved my life—I don't mean they saved me from hell, but they did save my sense of belonging. Ephesians 1:5-6 says that God adopted us into His family making us *"accepted in the Beloved."* When I discovered that in Jesus I am accepted and part of God's family, my esteem skyrocketed. God is my heavenly Father. He gave His only Son for my ransom. Now I am a joint heir with Christ and surrounded by other brothers and sisters in faith. That's family (Ephesians 3:15)! That is why being connected to a local church is so important.

At church, we fellowship together. We do life together and encourage one another to keep growing. It is wonderful to know there's a place where you're accepted and loved.

A SENSE OF VALUE

To build a healthy esteem, children need a solid understanding of their value and worth. The world can't give it to them, and family sometimes doesn't. Our culture does not understand the value of human life. They'll protect an eagle egg, but not an unborn child. They teach evolution and celebrate abortion and euthanasia without realizing the consequences of an entire generation believing those things are moral and good. So how do we develop a sense of value and worth in our children? We teach them to look at life from God's perspective.

No matter what we have experienced in life, we are extremely valuable to God (Matthew 6:25-26; 10:12,29)! He made us (Psalm 139:14; Ephesians 2:10). We are His. And He has good plans for us. Jeremiah 29:11, in the Jerusalem Bible says, *"I know the plans I have in mind for you. Plans of peace, non-disaster, reserving a future full of hope for you."* God's plans for us are good. He thinks only happy thoughts about us. He values us and wants us to see ourselves in the same way.

I know we don't always feel wonderfully or purposefully made, but that's why it is so important to teach our children how precious they are to God. God does not make mistakes. Even in the natural world, market forces of supply and demand determine the value of a thing. When there is a surplus of supply with little demand, the price goes down. When supply is limited and demand is high, the price goes up. That is how a free market works. If we translate that concept to our life, we all have something to offer this world. We are all unique. Your children have something to offer this world that no one else has. All they have to do is discover that unique purpose and use it to bless the world in a way only they can.

Rarity also determines value. Take antiques for instance. I used to think function determined value, but if that were true, why are antiques so expensive? Most of the time, they don't even work! Rarity is what determines price. I like old wagons and wagon wheels. (I think it's the spirit of adventure they represent.) If there were only one hundred original, wild-West wagons left, the price of each would be high. But if 50 of them were burnt in a fire, what would happen to the price? It would escalate. If something else happened and only 10 survived, none of us would be able to afford one!

How much more valuable are your children? There is nobody else on the planet like your child. When they struggle with the fear of not fitting in or being different (which everyone goes through), remind them that it is their uniqueness that gives them value. Encourage them to be themselves. They are like that wagon wheel—rare and of great worth in God's sight. When I say themselves, I'm not talking about a sinful perverted self. I'm talking about who God created them to be.

First Peter 1:19 says that we were not purchased or redeemed with corruptible things like silver or gold, but with *"the precious blood of Christ."* Does your child realize that? Do they realize that God paid for their redemption with the very life of His Son? Think about this: To you, a home's worth may exceed its monetary value, but how much is it worth to someone else? It's only worth what someone is willing to pay for it.

Our home is in a beautiful location; it's like a little piece of heaven, and right now, I could get three to four times what I paid for it. (It was such a blessing how God orchestrated getting it into our hands!) One day someone might offer me a million dollars for my place, but I'll not sell it. It's worth much more to me. That pales in comparison to how God values our kids. He didn't give a sheep or pigeon to redeem them. He sent Himself, Jesus Christ the sinless Son of God to pay the debt of sin. He bought us with His own life (Isaiah 59:16; John 3:16-18). Wow!

SELF-RESPECT

This concept of a person's intrinsic worth should inspire a healthy respect in our children—respect for God, respect for others whom God loves, and respect for themselves. One of the ways we can encourage this is by offering our respect to them. Mankind was created by God, in His image and likeness, and crowned with glory and honor (Psalm 8:4-6). John 5:44 says, *"How can you believe, who receive honor from one another, and do not seek the honor that comes from the only God?"* We were created for honor. The question is where and how we get it. In John 12:42-43, Jesus rebuked the Pharisees who wouldn't believe for fear of being cast out of the synagogues. *"They loved the praise of men more than the praise of God."*

We all crave honor. We crave praise. But we have to learn to get it from God. You can model this with your children and praise them for their accomplishments in life. Praise them for their morality and goodness. Praise them for reading their Bible or listening to biblical teaching. Remember, what we celebrate we elevate. If we don't honor our children and speak to them with respect, praising them for their accomplishments, they will look for that honor in the world. So, speak to your child with respect. Bless them and honor them for doing right. Show them who God is and how He praises them, then teach them to respect themselves.

A Sense of Competence

We live in a culture that tries to build people's esteem on feelings only. But God created us in His image. He created us to work. Work is part of the image of God in humankind (Genesis 1:27). For six days God worked. And on the seventh, He rested. If we do not work or create, we warp God's image within us. If we do not have something to conquer and overcome, we destroy our esteem.

Many people want a society with no losers or winners, one where everyone receives the same thing. We want to play sports, but we don't want to hurt anyone's feelings, so we don't keep score. That's crazy! God is a winner. The devil is a loser. And you can bet the kids are keeping score whether you do or not. "Yeah, but if they lose, they'll be sad." What's wrong with us? Life is full of successes and failures, and each one develops our character. *The more we try to level the playing field—to get rid of losers and winners, right and wrong, moral and immoral—the more we destroy people's personhood.*

Teach your children to get out of bed, do chores, and conquer short-term goals. One day they're going to need that experience to get and keep a job. They're going to need to know how to win graciously and how to handle defeat. They're going to need to know how to get back up and persevere through difficult circumstances.

Get your kids involved in sports, if they are athletic. Put them in dance classes if they like to dance or music lessons if they're interested in music. Get them into cheerleading or spelling bees or whatever they enjoy so they can develop esteem through a sense of accomplishment. Make sure they do their homework. Reward good grades; encourage improvement. They do not have to be straight-A students, but push them to do their best. If they are a C student, reward and praise the Cs, but shoot for Bs. If they earn a B, act like they hung the moon! Discover what your kids are good at or have a passion for and help them pursue it.

DEALING WITH PRESSURE

During the preparation phase, parents are also helping their children discover their gifts and talents, strengths and passions, and directing them toward their future careers. They are helping their children develop disciplines that will follow them for the rest of their lives, things like a good work ethic, study habits, and self-awareness. Parents should encourage teens in healthy esteem (especially their identification in Christ), making wise decisions, and healthy interpersonal relationships. All these things—the skills for today and a hope for the future—help children stand strong in the face of pressure.

Just remember (and prepare your children for the fact that) peer pressure never goes away. It doesn't end after high school or college like some people say or even hope. Pressure is something we all experience and have to learn to deal with throughout our lives. The earlier we learn to do that (while still under our father and mother's care) the more "natural" it will become to us. (I put the word *natural* in quotes, because this is really not a natural skill. It is a supernatural one—one that every believer is equipped with, but one that has to be exercised in order to see its fruit.) The three most common pressures we experience in life are peer pressure (friends), sexual pressure, and ungodly social norms (culture).

Peer Pressure

Proverbs 29:25 says that the fear of man brings a snare. It is a trap that kills our faith in God. John 5:44 says, *"How can you believe, who receive honor from one another, and do not seek the honor that comes from the only God?"* Caring more about what others think or say than what God thinks or says kills faith.

We must teach our children to process and overcome this type of pressure early in life so that their faith-obedience to God is not compromised. Giving in to the fear of people—whether through societal pressure in the media or on the job, politicians, or college professors and woke activists—will intimidate our children and push them into unrighteousness. Many godly parents panic when their children or teenagers have a faith crisis. But this is a good thing. If their faith is tested early (while still under your covering), you can help them process it properly. Then their faith has an opportunity to develop into a godly fear of the Lord. They will be able to stand for truth and righteousness instead of following the crowd of culture off a cliff. A faith crisis in adulthood has far greater repercussions than one in their teenage years.

Sexual Pressure

During adolescence, bodies are changing and hormones are raging. Sexual curiosity is normal. But at times the pressure to engage in premarital sex can feel overwhelming. As uncomfortable as it may be, teaching a biblical perspective of sexuality is vital during this time. We must share with our children the dangers of sex before marriage, but also—and this is not something the Church has done a good job of—we must teach them the beauty and pleasure God intended for sexual intimacy within the marriage covenant.

If, as parents, we don't teach them, their friends and the world will. Hebrews 13:4 says, *"Marriage is honorable among all, and the bed undefiled; but fornicators and adulterers God will judge."* This scripture covers both the blessing of sexual intimacy within the bounds of marriage and God's judgment on sexual immorality. First Corinthians 6:18 says, *"Flee sexual immorality. Every sin that a man does is outside the body, but he who commits sexual immorality sins against his own body."* All sins have a wage (Romans 6:23). But the wages of sexual sin come into the body. One of those consequences is venereal disease. HIV is still part of our world, and it is not the only consequence of sex outside marriage. But within marriage, God sanctifies our sexual activities and deems them wholesome and pleasurable. In other words, sex is amoral. Within God's boundaries of marriage it is good—outside it is bad.

When I was teaching my children about sex, I tried to help them understand this concept using the natural examples of water and fire. Both water and fire are amoral. They are neither good nor evil, but how we relate to each determines its effect on our lives. For example, you can't live three days without water, yet you can't live three minutes underneath it. Water within the bounds of a riverbank is a blessing. It brings life everywhere it flows. Outside those bounds, its floodwaters are destructive. In the boundaries of a fireplace, fire too is a blessing. It provides warmth to the whole house. It lights our homes and helps us cook. Outside that boundary, fire threatens all who live in (and out) of the home. If not contained, fire can threaten your family and even burn down an entire city. How would someone respond if you asked, "What do you think about fire?" It would depend on their history, right? Someone who has never been burnt or never lost anything in a fire would say, "Fire is good. I'm thankful for it." But to someone who lost their home in a fire, fire is bad. It is scary and dangerous. In reality, fire is just fire. What makes it good or bad is the relationship people have with it in or out of its boundaries. We see this principle demonstrated throughout scripture, and we must take the time to teach it to our children (Revelation 2:14; Numbers 22-23; Judges 16; 2 Samuel 11–12).

Friends

First Corinthians 15:33 is very clear, the company we keep plays a huge role in the trajectory of our lives. *"Do not be deceived. Evil company corrupts good habits."* Yet many are deceived about this. Parents expect their children to overcome the bad influence of their friends when, as adults, they struggle to stand firm in the face of peer pressure. How many adults cave in the workplace when their company celebrates pride month or when a coworker tells an inappropriate joke? We need to be more like the three Hebrew children who did not bow to societal pressure and turned the king's heart with their commitment to God (Daniel 3). How did they do this? One of the ways was the encouragement of their friends. They had each other. This is why it is so important that we continue to assemble as the body of Christ (Hebrews 10:25).

We need each other. We need good, mature, loyal-to-Jesus friends who can encourage us to stand strong and hold us accountable when we face temptation. Proverbs 13:20 (NLT) says, *"Walk with the wise and become wise; associate with fools and get in trouble."* As parents, we need to know who our children are hanging out with and where they are at all times. We also need to teach them how to choose godly friends. They will likely push the boundaries on this, and that's okay. But do not disengage. Kids need someone to help them make the hard decisions, and that someone is you. You are not their friend right now.

I'm not saying you can't have fun with your kids or that you should be anything other than kind and loving. But you are not their buddy or pal. (That comes in the adult stage.) You are their guardian, their protector and life coach. You have to teach your children to love others without participating in bad behaviors. You have to teach them the doctrine of separation (2 Corinthians 6:14-18). Children have to learn that there are certain people they need to avoid. Romans 16:17 says, *"...note those who cause divisions and offenses, contrary to the doctrine which you learned, and avoid them."*

15

THE POWER OF IDENTITY

Therefore, if anyone is in Christ, he is a new creation; old things have passed away; behold, all things have become new.
—*2 Corinthians 5:17*

Identity is who you are or who you believe yourself to be. It's your personality and personhood. It's what makes you unique. Dictionary.com defines *identity* as "the distinguishing character or personality of a person. The relationship established by psychological identification." In other words, who and what we identify with affects our identity. It affects how we view ourselves.

All of us have two dominant identifications that affect our eternity. The first is our identity in Adam. The second is our identity in Christ. In Adam, we are separated from God, lost and born into sin, which leads to death. This identity was not ours by choice. It was passed down to us through Adam's sin. However, our second identity works solely by choice. In Christ, we are born again into the family of God (John 3:3). We are saved from sin and made righteous, which leads to life. Our first identity or first birth is natural. It is of the flesh. Our second identity or new birth is supernatural. It is of the Spirit (John 3:5-6).

Everyone born in Adam suffers from identity crises. In every generation Satan works to exploit this crisis, and in ours has found a way to do so on a systemic level. He is using media, government, education, and medicine to push gender confusion and euphoria on our kids. If not countered, this dangerous assault on their personhood will destroy their future. Mutilating a child's body to "alter" their gender does not change their psychological or physiological makeup. Every cell in their body and blood is wired with either two X chromosomes (making them female) or an XY chromosome (making them male). No amount of artificial hormones will change that. What society is doing is child abuse. It robs children of their destinies as moms and dads.

God is the Author of our gender (Genesis 1:27; Psalm 139:13; Mark 10:6-7). And He doesn't make mistakes. Neither does He want us to be confused. We must ensure our children know how valuable they are—exactly as God created them (Ephesians 2:10). They need to know that God has a plan and purpose for their lives. And that part of His purpose is tied to their God-given gender, their gender assignment by Creator God.

God designs us and matches us to our purpose in our mother's womb (Psalm 139:13). Scripture says that Jeremiah, an Old Testament prophet, was separated unto his destiny in his mother's womb (Jeremiah 1:5). Paul was called and separated in his mother's womb to preach to the Gentiles (Galatians 1:15-16). John the Baptist was filled with the Spirit in his mother's womb to prepare the way of the Lord (Luke 1:15). God knew each of these men before they were born, and He crafted their identity—including their gender—to support the purpose He had for their lives.

Identity sets the course of our life. Who we believe we are affects every single one of our actions. It determines the kind of life we'll live. If we believe we're an accident, our actions will reflect that. Insecurity and inferiority nearly devoured me early in life. But pride and conceit can do the same thing. And while knowing who we are after the flesh—what we like, what we're good at, where we're weak, etc.—is important, God wants us to understand that is not all we are. His plans for us transcend what we can do naturally. They are tied to what He can do through us (Philippians 4:13).

This is why we need to introduce our children to Jesus early in life. When we are born again, we become new creations in Christ Jesus and the course of our life changes. Though we keep the same natural strengths and abilities, we are made righteous and now have the grace—the ability—to act like it. Righteous people do righteous things. As a Christian, everything we do comes from our identity in Christ. We are no longer broken. We are not accidents. We are whole—spirit, soul, and body (1 Thessalonians 5:23). But we will continue to live like we did in Adam unless we renew our minds to our new condition in Christ.

Our new identity in Christ is a finished work in our spirit. But to experience its benefits we have to agree with God. Do you see yourself as God sees you? Or do you only see yourself after the natural? How we see ourselves affects our esteem.

God loves us so much He gave Jesus to die for us. When we come to Him and call upon His name, He asks us to deny self, to take up our cross and follow Him. That means we have to stop seeing our old self in Adam. We have to recognize the paradoxical truth that while we can do nothing without Christ (as seen in John 15:5), as believers, we are never without Christ and can do all things through Him (Philippians 4:13). We must help our kids understand that humans connected to God, working with God, and allowing God to work through them can do all things. Independent of God, working outside His word, produces nothing of eternal value.

Depending on God, looking to God, listening to God, following God, and obeying God produces a healthy esteem. Independence and rebellion to God destroys esteem. That is because esteem comes from our internal sense of value and worth. When we know God loves us, chose us, and has a plan for our lives, we flourish in our divine design. When we do what is right, that too contributes to our esteem. When we violate our divine design, walk away from God, and choose to sin, we frustrate our esteem. Sin affects our sense of value. It makes us less than God ordained us to be.

Culture pushes our kids to build self-esteem independent of God. They want to feel good about themselves while shaking a fist at God. But this only leads to destruction—destruction of the "self" we are trying to elevate and destruction to our fellow man. Romans 7:18 says that *"...in me (that is, in my flesh) nothing good dwells...."* Why did Paul, the writer of Romans, qualify this statement with *"in my flesh"*? Because he knew that Christ dwelt in his born-again spirit, and that was a very good thing! According to Philemon 1:6, acknowledging this reality is what built Paul's faith, and it will build your child's faith as well.

You see, in Christ, our divine design is righteousness and love. When we do what is right, when we love God and people, it's amazing how good we feel. When we don't behave in a God-honoring way, we feel that, too. It hurts. We feel violated because we have violated our own design. Often we look at sin as simply moral or immoral. That's not how God sees it. He sees sin for the pain and death it brings. When you sleep with your neighbor's wife, you destroy part of your personhood. You bring death to yourself and to your neighbor (and to your kids, your neighbor's kids, your spouse, their spouse, etc., etc. The death just keeps going). If you steal your neighbor's stuff, it is wrong, but you also hurt yourself and your neighbor. Yes, sin is immoral, but it also damages our esteem and personhood. We need to help our kids understand this. We need to help them develop their Christ-esteem by teaching them who they are in Christ. (You can find more about this topic in my book *Identity Theft*.)

Only God's Word can reveal this Christ-identity to us. Scripture is like a mirror into the spiritual realm. When we look into the scripture, the Holy Spirit renews our minds to our new identity in Christ. Our lives are transformed by being conformed into that spiritual image. As believers, we should not have high *self*-esteem, but we should have high *Christ*-esteem. The self, our old self in Adam, is dead, and we have the power to deny its ability to lead us. Now, we are united to Christ in our spirit. And in that identity, we are more than conquerors (Romans 8:31-37)!

Help your children discover this new identity by looking up biblical phrases such as "in Him," "with Him," "through Christ," "in Christ," and "together with Christ" during your family devotions. For example, *"In Him we live and move and have our being… 'For we are also His offspring'"* (Acts 17:28). And, *"I can do all things through Christ who strengthens me"* (Philippians 4:13). Or, *"Now thanks be to God who always leads us in triumph in Christ, and through us diffuses the fragrance of His knowledge in every place"* (2 Corinthians 2:14).

16

RECREATIONAL DATING

Don't copy the behavior and customs of this world, but let God transform you into a new person by changing the way you think. Then you will learn to know God's will for you, which is good and pleasing and perfect.

—*Romans 12:2 NLT*

As children of God, we need to evaluate every custom our culture has to determine whether or not it is beneficial to our lives as believers. I love what the Message Bible says: *"Don't become so well-adjusted to your culture that you fit into it without even thinking. Instead, fix your attention on God. …Readily recognize what He wants from you, and quickly respond to it"* (Romans 12:2). Dating is a cultural custom that needs to be reevaluated as children of God.

Recreational dating is harmful to young people. Yet, I've discovered few over the years who are willing to buck the system and heed scripture's warning about this practice. Instead, they exalt cultural traditions and nullify the effects of God's Word in their children's lives (Mark 7:13). We need God's wisdom to navigate these troubled waters and help our children see its pitfalls. I pray you have an ear to hear (and eye to read) this chapter.

Dating is a societal tradition with no biblical foundation. In fact, many of its practices are forbidden in scripture. Recreational dating grows out of a boy-girl relationship in which they cultivate their interest in one another by pairing up and planning activities together, often without parental consent or oversight. These activities often involve them being alone together for extended periods of time "having fun." Where is wisdom in that?

Do teenagers (or adults) not face temptation? Are we hoping they will miraculously escape the pitfalls and negative consequences of such an arrangement? Why are we, as parents, abdicating our God-given responsibility to protect our children, know where they are, who they are with, and what they are doing? Do we not trust God's system of finding a mate and getting to the marriage altar?

Let's look at an example Jesus gave about elevating tradition above God's Word. In Mark 7:9-13, Jesus rebuked the Pharisees for teaching that it was okay to dishonor your parents in the context of giving or ministry.

> He said to them, "...you reject the commandment of God, that you may keep your tradition. For Moses said, 'Honor your father and your mother....' ...But you say, 'If a man says to his father or mother, "Whatever profit you might have received from me is"'...a gift to God, then you no longer let him do anything for his father or his mother, making the word of God of no effect through your tradition...."

It's never okay to dishonor your parents. Yet we allow recreational dating to dishonor parental rights for the "special rights" of teenagers.

Jesus also says we could judge a tree by its fruit. Does recreational dating have good or bad fruit associated with it (Matthew

12:33)? Does it facilitate sexual purity or compromise? Let's look at some of the pitfalls of dating.

PITFALLS OF DATING
REMOVES PARENTAL OVERSIGHT

Proverbs 16:25 (NLT) says, *"There is a path before each person that seems right, but it ends in death."* The custom of dating removes parents from the decision-making process of who our children spend time with and will eventually marry. It puts *feelings* firmly in the driver's seat. We don't have to look far to see the fruit of this pitfall. The divorce rate in our culture—even in the church—testifies of our inability to successfully discern who would make a good life partner. Though our feelings, at the time of decision, may be real, they are unreliable. Feelings come and go. They are easily manipulated and can quickly morph into something unrecognizable.

Everyone who enters into marriage says (and believes) they love each other. They all experience that emotional feeling of attachment. But because so many couples start their relationship based on only physical characteristics, they never develop soulical or spiritual connections. The world has things backward. God teaches us to start off with a spiritual connection, *"Do not be unequally yoked together with unbelievers"* (2 Corinthians 6:14). And then discover if we are soulically compatible. Do we have common goals and philosophies of life? Do we have similar likes and dislikes? Can we talk together? Do we enjoy being around each other? If we are both spiritually and soulically compatible, and we choose to marry, we will enjoy a lifetime of physical love as well.

In recreational dating, parents have very limited influence over who their child chooses to build relationship with. Think about that. Who our children marry is the most important decision of their lives, second only to following Jesus. It is a high-risk decision—not one we want them to make with only their emotions! Our children need to honor us in this process for things to go well (Ephesians 6:3). They need to see us as an ally, not an enemy. While I'm certainly not advocating for arranged marriages; I am a proponent of parental involvement in this process.

THREAT TO SEXUAL PURITY

Dating subjects our children to temptations even the mature fail to conquer. We're all weak after the flesh and subject to compromise, which is why Romans 13:14 says, *"But put on the Lord Jesus Christ and make **no provision** for the flesh, to fulfill its lust."* The easiest way to overcome temptation is to avoid it. So, as parents, we must ask ourselves: Does recreational dating make a provision for the flesh or for the spirit? Does it help our children *"flee sexual immorality"* (1 Corinthians 6:18)?

In 2 Timothy 2:22 (AMP), Paul instructs a young pastor to *"Run away from youthful lusts—pursue righteousness, faith, love, and peace with those [believers] who call on the Lord out of a pure heart."* In 1 Thessalonians 5:22 he says to *"Abstain from every form of evil."* And 1 Thessalonians 4:4-5 (NIV) says we should *"learn to control your own body in a way that is holy and honorable, not in passionate lust...."*

What I have seen of recreational dating does not allow our children to follow these scriptural mandates. I understand that most teenagers go into dating with good intentions. They want to remain pure and holy. But their flesh is weak (Matthew 26:41).

How many teens do you know that pray not to enter temptation before they go on a date? So why are we putting them in these situations?

Emotional Stability

Teens struggle with emotional stability. That's one of the symptoms of fluctuating hormones. Parents can help their children through this season with patience, understanding, and their consistent admonishment in the fruit of the Spirit. I had no assistance from my parents in this area, and the consequences of that followed me into dating. In ignorance, I participated in recreational dating as a teenager and created emotional drama in my own life and in the lives of several young girls'—from hookup to breakup. It was horrible. I'm thankful for God's forgiveness and healing, but parents need to be mindful of the emotional bonds created in dating. The greatest emotional pain in my life came from dating. Many teens struggle with depression, isolation, and suicidal thoughts when those emotional bonds get broken. In some cases, it is like they have experienced a mini divorce.

Spirituality

Dating and preoccupation with the opposite sex can hinder a teen's spiritual growth. Many young people think their teens are a time to pursue pleasure. They think they'll have plenty of time to seek God later, but it does not work that way. Ecclesiastics 12:1 says, *"Remember now your Creator in the days of your youth, before the difficult days come and the years draw near when you say, 'I have no pleasure in them.'"* The worldly philosophy of "sowing wild oats before settling down" in life is dangerous (Psalm 71:5, 71:17,

144:12; Matthew 19:20; Acts 26:4). It can take years to unravel the damage created during that time, and some damage may not be able to be reversed. How can you unsee what you've seen? There's always hope in God, but why not avoid the need for such a miracle?

Matthew 6:33 says, *"Seek first the kingdom of God and His righteousness...."* There is no age-appropriate clause attached to seeking God. We should all be learning to seek Him first. Not only will that action spare us from much pain and regret, but God promises that when we do, He will add "all these things" to us—one of which is a spouse. Proverbs 18:22 says that whoever finds a wife, finds a good thing and *"obtains favor from the Lord."* Instead of seeking a mate in dating, we should be seeking God and preparing to be the mate He wills us to be.

As parents, our job is to prepare our children for the future, a future that most likely includes a mate. We need to teach them to seek God first and trust Him to meet their needs. First Corinthians 7:27 asks, *"Are you bound to a wife? Do not seek to be loosed. Are you loosed from a wife? Do not seek a wife."* This simple principle refutes the world's preoccupation with hooking up. If you're married, do not seek a divorce. Even in adverse circumstances do all that is humanly possible to reconcile your differences and build a godly home and legacy. If you are single or divorced, do not seek a spouse. Seek God and trust Him to find a godly spouse who will be a blessing all the days of your life.

Ask yourself: When young people are actively seeking God, involved in church and youth group, does dating contribute to their spiritual growth? Or does it draw them away? Do they get more involved in church or less? What happens to their grades and other friendships? How about their relationship with you, their parents? These things are warning signs that their spiritual life is in jeopardy.

A THREAT TO FUTURE HAPPINESS

Nearly all the issues I deal with in marriage counseling are related to previous relationships a couple has had. Those other experiences tempt partners to compare their current relationship (both its challenges and expectations) with what has gone before. People have a tendency to drag their past into their present reality, and the hookup and breakup cycle of dating feeds into this. It bleeds over into marriage. Rather than committing to problem solving and communication, couples fall back on the quit-and-run pattern they established as a teen. They think *Peggy wouldn't be nagging me like this; I wish I was with Peggy.* What they don't realize is Peggy's husband is wishing for the same thing.

PROMOTES DECEITFULNESS

Becoming emotionally attached to someone in dating clouds judgment. The best place for young people to get to know someone of the opposite sex is in a group setting. People tend to be themselves in group settings and family gatherings. When they pair up and go off alone, deception begins. Both parties pretend to be something they are not to attract the other. But if a young man is "playing the field" before marriage, why would we be surprised by his lack of fidelity after marriage? If a young lady is clingy and selfish while dating, why would we expect something different after marriage?

This is yet another reason for parents to be involved in the dating and courting process. Parents know the strengths and weaknesses of their children, and they can often spot the strengths and weaknesses of whomever their child is dating. Many people enter marriage never really knowing the person they have chosen to wed. Often, they will be three-to-six months into the marriage before the real spouse shows up. Wouldn't it be better if our children got to know their spouses before their emotions got involved? Wouldn't it be better if they married a spouse for their character—not who they hoped the spouse would become?

Sexual Intimacy Is Expected

Recreational dating imposes on our children the cultural expectation of sexual intimacy. "Have you held hands yet?" middle schoolers ask their friends. "You didn't kiss her on the first date? How far did you get?" These days, it's not just girls who are pressured. Guys are too. There is an expectation for kids to see how far they can go. But the goal of dating should not be an exploration of sexuality. It should be to see if the other person has potential as a lifelong companion. It is to measure compatibility.

Much of this pressure originates in Hollywood. Movies picture the wonders of romance, but it is all smoke and mirrors. It's not real. While there must be attraction and chemistry in marriage, emotional, romantic love cannot be its foundation. Marriage is built on covenant. It is loyalty, commitment, and friendship-love. It is honor, respect, and dreams of a life built together (1 Peter 3:7). Romance is just the icing on the cake. If our children try to build their lives on nothing but ice, it will melt away. Their teenage crush will lead to being crushed, especially if they give in to the temptation of sexual intimacy.

Pregnancy and Other Long-Term Consequences

The pressure for sexual intimacy often leads to fornication (pre-marital sex) which, in turn, leads to other consequences. That's because physical intimacy is like a drug. It releases chemicals in the brain like dopamine and other endorphins that demand to experience a similar feeling over and over again. Sex also releases oxytocin, the bonding drug, connecting intimate partners in both body and soul.[1]

Sex outside marriage can lead to disease, emotional trauma, and unwanted pregnancy. In the United States, single moms are more likely to live in poverty than two-parent households. Children in these homes are also three-times more likely to experience abuse (often from "friends" of the family); ten times more likely to use drugs and alcohol; and 20 times more likely to go to jail.[2]

Abortion, in an unwanted pregnancy, is never an option, but I understand how plausible it can seem to a frightened, disillusioned teenager. With God's help, families and young mothers can overcome these circumstances, but there are no simple solutions. The best course of action is to implement precautions to avoid it.

We need to activate faith in God's plan for our children and teach them the joy of doing things God's way—marriage, good

---

1   Alyson Powell Key, Zilpah Sheikh, MD, reviewer, "What to Know About Oxytocin Hormone," *WEBMD,* September 8, 2024; https://www.webmd.com/sex-relationships/what-to-know-about-oxytocin; accessed March 26, 2025.

2   "Single Mom Statistics," *TheLifeOfASingleMom.com,* January 29, 2024; https://thelifeofasinglemom.com/single-mom-statistics-the-truth-about-single-moms; accessed March 26, 2025.

sex without these complications, and children. Our children can be light in a dark world. They can create a home with both a father and mother that will be a blessing to their children and grandchildren and continue the legacy of faith they inherit from us.

LAW OF DIMINISHING RETURNS

All sin progresses from one degree of darkness to another. First you lust, then lust leads to adultery. You hate and hate leads to murder. Sin is never satisfied. It simply gives place to greater and greater darkness (John 3:19; Matthew 8:12, 22:13, 25:30). Jesus once told a man who was healed, *"Sin no more, lest a worse thing come upon you"* (John 5:14). When we sin and refuse to repent, that sin becomes progressive. It goes from not good to bad to worse. Drugs are a good example. Marijuana is known as an entry-level drug for a reason. It offers a pleasurable high but also deadens the senses. People have to experiment with harder drugs to experience a similar feeling. Each high simply makes way for a new level of drug.

Sex is the same way. Where our children stop engaging in sexual intimacy today, they start tomorrow. It is like dynamite with a long fuse. Though no one has any intention of the dynamite going off, wherever the fuse is put out today is where it will light the next time. Eventually there won't be anything left of the fuse. It will just be dynamite.

Sex is a powerful force in our lives. Like playing with dynamite, there is no such thing as casual or safe sex. The only safe place for sexual love is marriage. First Corinthians 7:1 says, *"...It is good for a man not to touch a woman. Nevertheless, because of sexual immorality, let each man have his own wife and let each woman have her own husband."* Paul goes on to say that even married couples should not neglect their sexual relationship for long so Satan cannot tempt them.

What does Paul mean by not touching a woman? According to Strong's Concordance, this phrase means to "set a fire" or "kindle a flame" (G680, G681). Men have stronger sex drives than females, so anything that lowers a woman's restraints—anything that takes her from "No" to "Maybe" to "Okay"—is not good. If a woman's fire is kindled, it is all over but the shouting. And every lighting of the fuse gets her closer to that exploding piece of dynamite.

In all this, I'm not saying recreational dating is a sin. But it is unwise. It violates biblical warnings and often leads to unnecessary pain in our lives. In my personal experience, parents agree with the principles I've shared here, but many still allow dating by default. They see no alternative. Perhaps, as believers, we need to reconsider the traditional concepts of betrothal and courting that include parents in the decision-making process and take place in group settings.

17

FOUNDATIONS BY ADULTHOOD

> *So this is what the Lord God says: "See, I lay a stone in Zion, a tested stone, a precious cornerstone, a sure foundation; the one who believes will never be shaken."*
> —Isaiah 28:16 Berean Standard Bible

Remember Jesus' story of the wise and foolish builders told in Matthew 7:24-27? One man built his house on sand, the other on rock. Though both houses experienced similar weather phenomena, one fell while the other stayed standing. The difference? Their foundations. The same is true in our lives. Without a solid foundation, we will not survive the storms of life. Our children need those foundations as well, and it is our job, as parents, to provide them. Our children should not leave home without a basic understanding of who God is, who they are in Christ, and what they have been called to do (and be) in partnership with Him. But if we don't have these basic foundations laid by the time they are 20, it's too late.

At 20, our children are adults. They have been through the training and teaching phases with us, and now, it is time for them to transition into adulthood. As adults, they are responsible and held accountable to God for their actions. This phase can be hard for parents who have mixed up the order of stages and tried to be their child's friend (instead of a parent) too early. Now they don't know if their children are ready to leave the nest.

But by adulthood, whether we are ready for it or not, we must transition from relating to our children as parents to being their friend and life coach, which means giving advice only when our children ask for it. As adults, we also have to recognize their right to accept or reject our advice without censure. They do not dishonor us if they make a decision different from what we would make or if they feel God leading them another way; we are no longer accountable to God for their life choices.

Before getting to that stage, we must lay the foundation for our children's success by ensuring they do not leave home without these basic understandings:

- God loves you.
- God is for you.
- The fear of the Lord.
- Authority of scripture.
- Healthy esteem.
- Good work ethic.
- Financial stewardship.
- Repentance and forgiveness.
- Preparation for marriage.
- Prayer.

Let's delve into each more specifically:

GOD LOVES YOU.

All have sinned and need a Savior, yet God loves us. God's love was manifest on the Cross when Jesus died for our sins and rose for our justification. Our children must understand the importance of turning from sin and confessing Jesus as Lord of their life—without it, all else is forfeited (Romans 10:8-10). They need to know that God's kind of love is unconditional, unmerited, and intentional. There is nothing good they can do to get Him to love them more; nor is there any bad they can do that will cause Him to love them less. A knowledge of God's deep and abiding love for us causes our faith to work (Galatians 5:6). It casts out fear and allows us to run boldly to Him in our time of need (1 John 4:18; Hebrews 4:16).

GOD IS FOR YOU.

God is good and He has good plans for each of His children—plans to prosper us, not to harm us; plans for our future success (Jeremiah 29:11). No matter what happens in life, God is for our children; not against them (Romans 8:31). He does not punish us as our sins deserve (Psalm 103:10; Galatians 3:13; Romans 8:1-4). He is faithful to us. Even in discipline, He only desires our good (Hebrews 12:5-6). We cannot be too redundant in teaching these things to our children.

THE FEAR OF THE LORD.

A healthy, wholesome fear of the Lord is essential to our faith. But this fear is not tormenting. It is not a fear of wrath or rejection (2 Timothy 1:7; 1 John 4:16-18). The fear of the Lord is a reverence for who He is as Creator God (Job 1:20; Matthew 4:10; Deuteronomy 6:13). It is to be awestruck by His power, goodness, faithfulness, and mercy. It is worship. Jesus operated in this kind of fear, and so must we (Isaiah 11:2). A wholesome fear of God is the beginning of wisdom and knowledge (Proverbs 1:7, 2:5). To fear the Lord is to hate evil (Proverbs 8:13). Proverbs 10:27 says the fear of the Lord prolongs our days on the earth. It gives us confidence and provides us with refuge (Proverbs 14:26-27). And Job 28:28 says, *"...Behold, the fear of the Lord, that is wisdom, and to depart from evil is understanding."*

AUTHORITY OF SCRIPTURE.

Our children also need to know that God's Word is the final authority. It is unbiased truth that endures forever (Matthew 24:35). The Word of God sanctifies us (John 17:17). It sets us free and gives us direction in life (John 8:31-32; Psalm 119:105). The Word delivers us from destruction and brings healing (Psalm 107:20). My children learned their ABCs with scripture. In preschool, their teacher taught them that:

A – All have sinned and come short of the glory of God.
B – Believe on the Lord Jesus Christ and you will be saved.
C – Children obey your parents in the Lord for this is right.

This continued all the way through the letter Z. Our children still remember them and are teaching them to our grandchildren! Once, when our oldest daughter was about 6, we were eating with a pastor and his leaders, one of whom asked our daughter what she was learning in school. She stood up and quoted the alphabet with scriptures, from A to Z. The table was so impressed they (and other eavesdropping patrons in the restaurant) clapped for her accomplishment. Her face was beaming! Her mom and I were pretty proud, too! Never underestimate the power of God's Word planted in a sensitive heart. It will produce a harvest (1 Corinthians 3:6).

Healthy esteem.

Every child should know their value—both to God and their parents—before leaving home. I'm not promoting a healthy self-esteem in the sense of pride or arrogance in oneself. But neither am I advocating for a negative self-image. Self is the root of pride, and pride is the impetus of sin. But God doesn't want us living in low self-esteem. He doesn't want us living in *self* at all. We are worth more to Him than that (Romans 5:8).

God has called us to a high Christ-esteem. We were all born into Adam with a fallen identity; and before Christ, we all struggle with identity confusion. But today, confused adults are preying on children and imposing their sin on them. They are creating and affirming gender confusion in kids and giving them the authority to mutilate their bodies with reconstructive surgeries and hormone blockers. That is crazy! We need to protect our children from such foolishness—not by removing them from the world, but by teaching them their new identity in Christ. A positive Christ-image helps us deny self, take up our cross, and follow Jesus (Matthew 16:24). Before our children leave home, they need to know who they are in Christ and be able to separate their identity from their performance so they can keep growing in their knowing of what it means to be God's child.

GOOD WORK ETHIC.

By 20, our children need to know how to work and provide for themselves (2 Thessalonians 3:6-12). Work is part of God's image in us. In the beginning, God worked six days, and on the seventh, He rested (Genesis 2:2). We follow the pattern He set by working and resting as well. In the Garden, the first thing God gave Adam was a job (Genesis 2:19). Working is part of our worship to God (Colossians 3:17). It's how we *have* so that we can *give* (Ephesians 4:28). Mankind is less than human when we don't work. But our work is not to be done for people's praise. We work as to the Lord (Colossians 3:23; Ephesians 6:6-8). Our children must learn to earn their own way through work and do their best in all things to bring honor to God. *"Now those who are* [lazy busybodies] *we command and exhort through our Lord Jesus Christ that they work in quietness and eat their own bread"* (2 Thessalonians 3:12). Work contributes to our healthy esteem. It provides for us and future families, and it blesses the community at large.

FINANCIAL STEWARDSHIP.

Finances are not just carnal. They are spiritual. Children need to learn how to handle natural things so they can handle spiritual things well. *"He who is faithful in what is least* [finances] *is faithful also in much; and he who is unjust in what is least is unjust also in much"* (Luke 16:10). Before our children leave home, they need to know what God says about giving, tithing, sowing, savings, and storehouses; and they need to practice what His Word says. They need to understand that biblical prosperity is a partnership. God promises to provide, but we, in faith, partner with Him in stewardship.

Get money into your child's hands early and start teaching them how to handle it. Teach them to tithe as a "first fruit" of their increase and teach them to give what they have as a seed sown. When they do that, God will see their faith and reward it by blessing their storehouses and investments (Proverbs 3:9-10). Years ago, before one of my children had a job and access to their own money, they asked if they could give an extra pair of shoes to someone at school who needed them. Absolutely! I broke out in a happy dance that day because my child was learning to conquer covetousness. Covetousness is idolatry (Colossians 3:5). But giving breaks its foothold.

Teaching children to deny self, pray and believe, save their money, and work toward their goals are important life skills. It makes them master over their money instead of allowing money to master them (Matthew 6:22-24). And when they see God's faithfulness to keep His Word as they give, their faith will grow. Thanksgiving will well up in their hearts and further guard them from idolatry.

Repentance and forgiveness.

Everyone needs to know how to forgive. And everyone needs to know how to humble themselves and repent. Repentance is the road to transformation. It's what mind renewal is all about—a change of mind and direction (Romans 12:2). Unforgiveness and offense are two of Satan's biggest weapons, so let's not be ignorant of his devises (2 Corinthians 2:11). Teach your children to say, "I'm sorry," and teach them to forgive others whether or not they receive an apology. Don't let bitterness defile you or your children (Hebrews 12:15). Teach them to repent quickly when they mess up and forgive others when they are wronged (Matthew 6:12).

Preparation for Marriage.

Two of the biggest decisions we make in life are submitting to Jesus as Lord and choosing who to marry. We've already talked about the importance of introducing your children to Christ early in life and teaching them to grow and develop in His Word and the leading of the Holy Spirit. This training in hearing His voice and walking by faith will help them when they decide whom to marry. They won't base that decision solely on their feelings or what they see with their physical eyes. During their adolescent years, get your children involved in supervised group activities with people of the opposite sex. Things like youth group, youth camp, and conferences can rub some of the rough edges off their communication and social skills. Invite groups of teens to your house for game nights, backyard BBQs, and movie nights. Monitor how they relate to their peers, and in private times, teach them the skills they are missing. The teen years are awkward, but that is just part of the learning process.

Prayer.

No one inherently knows how to pray. We have to be taught. John taught his disciples to pray and Jesus taught His as well (Luke 11:1-4). And we need to teach our children to pray. Children learn by example. They also learn through direct teaching. In prayer, they need both. Pray with your children. Pray over them. Bless them and let them hear you. (I have several free resources to help you with this; you can find them on my website or by calling our helpline. Ask for "Blessing Your Children" and "The Fundamentals of Prayer.") Leverage special moments to teach prayer: Bedtime, mealtime, before tests or school presentations, after they've been hurt, etc. And teach them the model prayer that Jesus used to teach His disciples to pray:

> Our Father in heaven, hallowed be Your name. Your kingdom come. Your will be done on earth as it is in heaven. Give us this day our daily bread. And forgive us our debts, as we forgive our debtors. And do not lead us into temptation but deliver us from the evil one. For Yours is the kingdom and the power and the glory forever. Amen (Matthew 6:9-13).

Keep things simple and short. But engage with them in prayer in their everyday life and show them how relevant faith can be.

TIPS FOR TEENAGE YEARS

When my children were younger, they asked a lot of questions. But sometime during their teenage years, the questions stopped. My wife and I had to initiate questions to stay engaged in their lives. We had to draw them out to understand what they were thinking and how they were processing experiences so we could learn what they needed to help them keep growing.

The key during this time is relationship. Help your children learn to build healthy relationships both in and out of the home. But don't forget to practice what you preach. Be a good example and role model in this area. And have fun together. The following are a few ways Sue and I kept our family growing together during these years:

- We made our home the hangout place. When our kids were at home, we knew they were safe and having fun with their friends. We also got to know their friends and could see if and when we needed to redirect them in the choosing/maintaining of healthy relationships.

- We taught our children that as long as they were having a positive impact on their friends, they could remain friends. Whenever a friend began having a negative impact on our child, we helped them see they had moved into an unhealthy relationship.
- We had the local pizza place on speed dial.
- We stocked up on good movies and popcorn.
- We planned fun family nights.
- We sometimes took our kids' friends with us on mini vacations.

One thing we didn't have to do with our kids but have had to do with our grandchildren is to supervise their digital space. Digital addiction is real, so control the amount of time your children spend on tech/media platforms. First Corinthians 6:12 (NLT) tells us that while everything is permissible, not everything is beneficial. *"…even though 'I am allowed to do anything,' I must not become a slave to anything."* Inappropriate images, text messages, and comments can damage their developing brains and affect them for years to come. It's important to teach kids that no digital space is private—not only in your home as you strive to protect them, but also in the world. Things posted on social media today can be used against them tomorrow. Their brains are not fully developed. They don't always know when they are veering off into dangerous territory.

Teach your children to make good friends (and wise decisions) during this season. Proverbs 18:24 (NLT) tells us, *"There are 'friends' who destroy each other, but a real friend sticks closer than a brother."* And in those awkward times of struggle with friends, remind them that Jesus is our Friend who sticks closer than a brother.

Encourage them to keep treating people the way they wish to be treated, not the way they are treated (Luke 6:31). Don't retaliate when things go wrong. Don't double down to force someone's apology. Teach them to recognize that we can't control other people's actions. We can only control our own. Remember God's commandment to *"Love your neighbor as yourself"* (Leviticus 19:18). Remind them to hold tight to the truth that no matter what someone does or doesn't do; says or doesn't say—they have a choice. *"Even if everyone else is a liar, God is true"* (Romans 3:4 NLT). Their friend's behavior will never nullify God's faithfulness.

Transitioning

Be very careful, then, how you live—not as unwise but as wise, making the most of every opportunity, because the days are evil.
—*Ephesians 5:15-16 NIV*

18

DIFFERENT KINDS OF LOVE

Let love be without hypocrisy. Abhor what is evil. Cling to what is good.

—*Romans 12:9*

Much confusion exists in our culture over *love*. The world's version of love is sensual and self-gratifying. They use the word to express so many emotions, it has thus become descriptive of nothing. Unfortunately, believers have adopted similar behaviors. We say: "I love ice cream!" "I love the Dallas Cowboys!" "I love my dog." "I love my wife." (Whether you've used those expressions or not, I pray there is a difference between the love you have for your dog and that of your wife. And it better not be more love for your dog!)

Love is vital to every person's development and relationships. It's part of our common language as humans. But most Christian parents are not prepared to teach their children the biblical definition of *love*. When their teen or young adult asks, "How do I know when I'm in love?" parents fumble. They don't know how to respond. But as our children transition out of our homes, they need to know what love looks like so they can learn to recognize it in their own lives and actions and in the actions of others (1 Corinthians 13:4-8; Titus 2:4; 1 Thessalonians 4:9).

In Jesus' day, the Greeks and philosophers used at least seven different words to describe love: *agape, philia, eros, storge, philautia, ludus, pragma*. Let's examine each:

1. **Agape** – the selfless love of God. Agape is who God is. It is the highest form of love; the type of love God has for us, wills to reproduce in us, and works through us (Romans 5:5-8; 1 John 4:19). Agape is an unconditional, unmerited, and unoccasioned love. It is based on God's character and actions, not our conduct or emotions. Agape doesn't depend on any other type of love. It can be expressed to God, one another, or even strangers. Agape is connected to the concept of altruism and in the King James version of scripture is translated as *charity*. Agape is the practice of unselfish concern for another. It is the foundation for the other kinds of love and gives longevity to each. Agape is what causes us to reach our full potential.

2. **Philia** – is an affectionate, friendship love. Sometimes people call it "brotherly love." Philia is an emotional bond characterized by loyalty and trust. It can be shared among friends or family members. Philia is encouraging, kind, and thoughtful. It is a platonic, yet meaningful love; something that is purely spiritual and wholesome, completely free from sensual desire. First Samuel 18:1 talks about this special kind of love in the friendship between Jonathan and David: *"…the soul of Jonathan was knit to the soul of David, and Jonathan loved him as his own soul."* In philia, we truly value others. We cheer others on toward success and prosperity without envy or jealousy. In

philia, people often share common interests and simply enjoy being in one another's company.

3. **Eros** – a romantic, passionate, physical love that expresses itself through sexuality. This type of love was named after the Greek god of love, Eros. (In Rome, his name was Cupid.) According to myth, Eros' golden arrows were responsible for making people "fall in love." They were struck with uncontrollable feelings of physical attraction, passion, and lust. Basically, Eros made lovers victims. They could fall into and out of this type of love as easily and unpredictably as a bee taking flight. Scripture, however, says eros needs boundaries. It is dangerous when exercised outside them. Though Hollywood makes millions of dollars on exalting this kind of love, long-lasting relationships are not built on eros. It is part of, and reserved for, marriage; but it is not the foundation (Hebrews 13:4; 1 Corinthians 7:2-5). The best form of eros is built on the foundation of philia. That's what makes it sustainable.

4. **Storge** – familial love. This is the unconditional love a father and mother have for their children. Storge is protective and nurturing. It is one-sided (even if a child does not reciprocate love) and benevolent; it expects nothing in return. Storge sees and meets the needs of another, protects the other, and remains faithful to them no matter how much that person irritates you.

5. **Philautia** – Self-love. This kind of love must be kept in balance. It can be healthy when surrendered to Christ, but it easily becomes narcissistic when left to itself. Philautia is self-care. Think about the last time you flew on a plane. When the flight attendants go over safety procedures, what do they say about the oxygen mask? Put your own mask on before assist-

ing another, even a child. That feels wrong, but the message is "we can't give what we don't have." We have to take care of ourselves to be a blessing to others (Matthew 22:39).

6. **Ludus** – Playful, flirtatious love. Ludus is that feeling of carefree attraction that comes with infatuation. It is a shallow, zero-commitment type of love that can easily lead to no good. In Latin, *ludus* means to play, as in a game. If left unchecked, it often devolves into seduction and "casual sex." But there is nothing casual about sex.

7. **Pragma** – Committed, long-lasting love. Pragma is the opposite of ludus. It is an enduring, "tough it out" sort of love that thinks long-term. Pragma is about commitment, companionship, and dreams of the future. It is often an extension of agape love in the home and holds the mindset of "through patience and sacrifice, together, we can make it work."

With only one word in the English language to cover all these ideas, you can see why *love* has become so problematic. But in healthy, Christ-centered relationships, none of these loves are meant to be exclusive of one another. They work together with Agape as the foundation.

> *Beloved, let us love one another, for* **love is of God**; *and everyone who loves is born of God and knows God. He who does not love does not know God, for God is love* (1 John 4:7-8).

Agape love is not of this world. It does not come from the flesh; nor does it depend on our feelings. But it does affect our feelings in a positive, productive way. God's kind of love has to be taught (1 Thessalonians 4:9; Titus 2:4). It is not something that falls from the sky or rides on the tip of an arrow. Love grows as we grow in relationship with the Lord.

During Jesus' ministry someone asked:

> *"Teacher, which is the great commandment in the law?" Jesus said to him, "'You shall love the Lord your God with all your heart, with all your soul, and with all your mind.' This is the first and great commandment. And the second is like it: 'You shall love your neighbor as yourself.' On these two commandments hang all the Law and the Prophets"* (Matthew 22:36-40).

In other words, the entire message of the Bible is summed up in this: Love God and love your neighbor as yourself. But if we don't love God first, we cannot love people with His kind of love.

By the time our children reach 20 years of age, our goal should be for them to love God and esteem others, including their siblings and future spouse. What does that look like? According to Romans 13:10, *"love does no harm to a neighbor, therefore love is the fulfillment of the law."* That doesn't mean love won't speak up when it sees evil. Jesus was God made flesh, and though He didn't condemn us over sin, neither did He condone or celebrate it. He warned us of the wrath to come and gave us a way out (Matthew 11:20-24; John 8:11; John 5:14). First Corinthians 13:6 says that God's kind of love does not rejoice in iniquity; rather it rejoices in truth.

GOD'S LOVE

Let's look at some truths about God's love.

God's Love Is Taught, Not Caught.

But we don't need to write to you about the importance of loving each other, for God himself has taught you to love one another (1 Thessalonians 4:9 NLT).

God teaches us to love through His Word and Spirit. The world views love as a romantic, euphoric feeling. But God loves with action and in truth (1 John 3:18). What is truth? God's Word (John 17:17, 8:31-32). So, if we want to love like God, we must treat one another as directed in His Word.

Love Is of God, Not of This World.

First John 4:7-8 (NLT) says, *"Dear friends, let us continue to love one another, for love comes from God. Anyone who loves is a child of God and knows God. But anyone who does not love does not know God, for God is love."*

Human beings cannot love independent of God. Any "love" we see outside relationship with and knowledge of God is not God's kind of love. It is a poor imitation at best. To love with God's kind of love, we have to know Him and be born of Him. This is why scripture teaches us to marry other believers (2 Corinthians 6:14). To marry outside the community of faith is to go into full-time missionary work. A lost spouse cannot love with God's kind of love. It's not in them.

Love Is Revealed in the Cross.

God showed how much he loved us by sending his one and only Son into the world so that we might have eternal life through him. This is real love—not that we loved God, but that he loved us and sent his Son as a sacrifice to take away our sins (1 John 4:9-10 NLT).

Jesus' sacrifice was a demonstration of God's love (Romans 5:8). He loved us when we didn't deserve it, and He continues to love us though we can never earn it. God's love never runs out (Jeremiah 31:3).

GOD'S LOVE IS PERCEIVED.

It is known by revelation. We do not always feel God's love. But we can always see it in His acts of kindness and compassion. "*Hereby perceive we the love of God, because he laid down his life for us: and we ought to lay down our lives for the brethren*" (1 John 3:16 KJV). In our culture, we have reduced love to an uncontrollable emotion—something that just happens, like a virus. But God's love is not like that. His love is a choice demonstrated in words and actions that others can perceive.

LOVE SEES A NEED AND SUPPLIES IT.

When Abraham arrived at Mount Moriah to offer Isaac in obedience to God, Isaac asked where the sacrifice was. Abraham replied,

> *God will provide for Himself the lamb for a burnt offering* (Genesis 22:8).

> *Abraham lifted his eyes and looked, and there behind him was a ram caught in a thicket.... Abraham called the name of the place, The-Lord-Will-Provide; as it is said to this day, "In the Mount of the Lord it shall be provided"* (Genesis 22:13-14).

God sees and God provides because of His love. In parenthood, love sees and provides for the physical, emotional, intellectual, and spiritual needs of our children; and love teaches our children to perceive and meet the needs of others.

LOVE SACRIFICES.

It serves. As Jesus' earthly ministry was coming to a close, He was celebrating Passover with His disciples. John says that Jesus, knowing Judas (His betrayer) was sitting at the table with Him, rose up, laid aside His garments, and began to wash His disciples' feet (John 13).

> ...when Jesus knew that His hour had come...having loved His own who were in the world, He loved them to the end (John 13:1).

Jesus also knew Peter would deny Him. He knew the others would forsake Him. Yet, *"He loved them to the end."* What amazing love! This is the kind of love God has called each of us to have for our children and to teach our children to have for their families.

There is no such thing as a *family* independent of sacrifice. We sacrifice time, money, food, and preferences. Sacrifice upon sacrifice. I see people all the time making decisions to uproot their families, taking their kids out of good schools or their families away from a good church, to move across the country for an additional $5,000 or $6,000 a year. That is not love. Love makes itself available. It puts others' needs above their own and is loyal to the end. We have to learn to sacrifice things for the good of our homes, or we will sacrifice our homes for more things.

GOD'S LOVE IS STEADFAST AND UNCONDITIONAL.

God's love is based on His character, not our conduct. God loved us when we were His enemies, and He proved that love in the gift of His Son (Romans 5:8-10). Now who (or what) can separate us from that love? Can hardship? Threats? Persecution? Lack? Danger? Pain or war? No! In all these things, His love helps us overcome (Romans 8:35-37).

> *For I am persuaded that neither death nor life, nor angels nor principalities nor powers, nor things present nor things to come, nor height nor depth, nor any other created thing, shall be able to separate us from the love of God which is in Christ Jesus our Lord* (Romans 8:38-39).

While we never condone sin in another, loving them with God's kind of love means we also do not allow it to separate us from them. In a world where love is hypocritical and selfish, our love must be a shining example of the love of God. It must remain steadfast.

GOD'S LOVE ACCEPTS US WHERE WE ARE BUT NEVER GIVES UP ON OUR ABILITY TO CHANGE.

People hurt us, sometimes intentionally. But God's love sustains us, and His love in us helps us separate what a person does from who they are. It allows us to keep loving, even in the hurt, and believe in their ability to learn and grow. When we excel in love like that, even in correction, we express who God is and give the other person a chance to know Him.

Love forgives.

The purpose of God sending His Son was forgiveness and reconciliation (John 3:16-17). That is the heart of love—relationship. Never be too proud to ask for forgiveness, and do not withhold forgiveness from anyone. As believers, we should always work toward reconciliation. That doesn't mean we put ourselves into dangerous situations, but we leave the door open for God's grace to work.

And be kind to one another, tenderhearted, forgiving one another, even as God in Christ forgave you (Ephesians 4:32).

While we can't force others to reconcile, we can keep our heart right toward them. We can forgive our own mistakes and leave the door open for God to work in both people's lives.

19

SEXUAL PURITY

Let there be no sexual immorality, impurity, or greed among you. Such sins have no place among God's people.
—*Ephesians 5:3 NLT*

It is amazing to me how confused the average Christian seems to be about sexual purity. Ephesians 5:5-6 (NLT) tells us:

You can be sure that no immoral, impure, or greedy person will inherit the Kingdom of Christ and of God. For a greedy person is an idolater, worshiping the things of this world. Don't be fooled by those who try to excuse these sins, for the anger of God will fall on all who disobey him.

Our culture may be fooled over this issue, but you and I are not appointed for wrath (Romans 5:8-9; 1 Thessalonians 1:10). We are saved from the wrath to come, and because we are saved, we need to put these old practices away (Ephesians 4:22, 5:8-9).

God is very specific about the boundaries of our sexuality. He designed sex for marriage. Within that boundary, sex is precious. It is pleasurable. It bonds a husband and a wife together for a lifetime. But outside that boundary sex is dangerous. That's why scripture says, *"But among you there must not be even a hint of sexual immorality or of any kind of impurity, or of greed, because these are improper for God's holy people"* (Ephesians 5:3 NIV).

In Galatians, as Paul outlines the difference between the works of the flesh and the fruit of the Spirit, he calls us to be sober, honest, and authentic. He tells us to recognize our tendency toward weakness. No one is beyond failing. We all deal with temptation, but as believers we are also equipped to overcome.

When we walk after the Spirit, scripture says we will not fulfill the lust of the flesh (Galatians 5:16). Scripture doesn't say, if we walk after the Spirit our flesh will not lust. We will simply not fulfill it. If we quit pursuing God, yielding to Him, and walking by faith, we will fall. We will begin fulfilling the work of the flesh, from the pulpit to the pew. If a preacher ever thinks he or she is beyond failing, they stop guarding against that possibility and do eventually fail in their sexuality (Proverbs 16:18). For myself, I know I am susceptible to sexual immorality. That's why I guard against it and how I know I will likely never fall into it. I recognize that I am not above it.

In 2 Corinthians 12:19-21 Paul instructs the church in the importance of sexual purity by calling for repentance. He says, *"…we do all things, beloved, for your edification. For I fear…I shall mourn for many who have sinned before and have not repented of the uncleanness, fornication, and lewdness which they have practiced."* Repentance is a change of mind and direction. When a person realizes they have been walking after the flesh in their sexuality, or any other sin, and they repent, that doesn't just mean they are sorrowful. It means they turn around and begin following after the Spirit. And that is what gives them the power—or grace—to leave sin behind.

Galatians says when we identify with, habitually practice, and celebrate the works of the flesh, we will not inherit God's kingdom.

Now the works of the flesh are evident, which are: adultery, fornication, uncleanness, lewdness, idolatry, sorcery, hatred, contentions, jealousies, outbursts of wrath, selfish ambitions, dissensions, heresies, envy, murders, drunkenness, revelries, and the like; of which I tell you beforehand, just as I also told you in time past, that those who practice such things will not inherit the kingdom of God (Galatians 5:19-21).

First Corinthians 6:9-10 (NLT) tells us the same thing:

Don't you realize that those who do wrong will not inherit the Kingdom of God? Don't fool yourselves. Those who indulge in sexual sin, or who worship idols, or commit adultery, or are male prostitutes, or practice homosexuality, or are thieves, or greedy people, or drunkards, or are abusive, or cheat people— none of these will inherit the Kingdom of God.

But Paul goes on to write, *"Some of you were once like that. But you were cleansed; you were made holy; you were made right with God by calling on the name of the Lord Jesus Christ and by the Spirit of our God"* (1 Corinthains 6:11 NLT). Our new identity in Christ frees us from the power of sin. These things were not just things we did; they were who we were in Adam. Now we are in Christ—forgiven and made righteous and truly holy (Ephesians 4:24).

What would you think if I said it's okay to hate one another or worship idols? Hopefully, you'd think, *You're crazy!* So why do we fall for the lie when culture says, "Adultery can be healthy. It can add spice to a marriage," or "Kids are going to experiment with sex, just make sure it is safe"? All those practices are works of the flesh; we overcome them by walking after the Spirit. And if we fall, we repent quickly. We do not celebrate sin because we are no longer sinners. We aren't children of darkness. We are children of God. First John 1:9 says, to believers, *"If we confess our sins, He is faithful and just to forgive us our sins and to cleanse us from all unrighteousness."* When we fail as children of God, we need to be quick to repent and receive God's mercy and forgiveness. We need to turn around and keep walking after the Spirit because that is who we are.

If you have participated in sin, any sin—hatred, gossip, idolatry, homosexuality, adultery, fornication, or anything else listed in Galatians and 1 Corinthians—you can experience forgiveness and cleansing by calling upon the name of the Lord. You can be washed. You can quit living in that old way and begin to live in the new way of the Spirit. And you will fulfill God's plan and will for your life and marriage.

It is not a lack of love for me to command the homosexual, adulterer, or fornicator to repent. Just like it is not a lack of love that commands the thief or gossiper to repent. Anyone doing anything contrary to sound doctrine, "Repent!" Call on the name of the Lord and be forgiven. If you fail, repent, and get back up. Keep following the way of the Spirit. You may be tempted as a Christian. You may even make a mistake, but don't live there or glory in it. That's not who you are. You are a child of God, so act like it.

"But I can't help it," some say. "I was born this way." Then get born again and put away those old practices. If you are born again, remember who you are in Christ. You have no right to sin.

*Do you not know that your bodies are members of Christ? Shall I then take the members of Christ and make them members of a harlot? Certainly not! Or do you not know that he who is joined to a harlot is one body with her? For "the two," He says, "shall become one flesh." But he who is joined to the Lord is one spirit with Him. Flee sexual immorality. Every sin that a man does is outside the body, but he who commits sexual immorality sins against his own body. Or do you not know that your body is the temple of the Holy Spirit who is in you, whom you have from God, and **you are not your own**? For you were bought at a price; therefore glorify God in your body and in your spirit, which are God's* (1 Corinthians 6:15-20).

Again, new life in Christ does not mean we will never face temptation. Everyone is tempted. Temptation is not a sin. Just because you're tempted in an area doesn't mean you are that sin. Some people have a predisposition to alcoholism, and the devil can tempt them in that area. But that does not make them an alcoholic. They have to follow temptation with action and continue in it to become an alcoholic. First Corinthians 10:13 says, *"No temptation has overtaken you except such as is common to man; but God is faithful, who will not allow you to be tempted beyond what you are able, but with the temptation will also make the way of escape, that you may be able to bear it."*

God always provides a way out of temptation, but even if we fail, He still loves us. He does not pour His wrath on us or curse us as if we were still under the law (Galatians 3:13; Romans 8:1-4). There are still consequences to sin. There always is. But that doesn't disqualify us to be God's children. Were I to participate in sexual sin, it could destroy my marriage. It could destroy my kids, my friendships and influence. But that wouldn't mean I'm no longer called by God. God's gifts and call are irrevocable (Romans 11:29). However, sin will hinder my impact and influence.

Our sexuality needs to be under control (1 Corinthians 6:12). Promiscuity and perversion cause lust to explode in our hearts. They possess us and without repentance will begin to control our lives. But our bodies don't belong to sin. They don't even belong to us. Our bodies belong to the Lord. They are the temple of the Holy Spirit (1 Corinthians 6:19-20).

The world will lie to our children about their bodies. Politicians, college professors, friends, and even other family members will tell them they have a right to do what they please with their bodies—from sexual immorality to abortion. But scripture is clear. Our bodies were bought with a price—the precious blood of Jesus. We must prepare our children for the deception they will face in this world by teaching them that their bodies belong to God and their future mate (1 Corinthians 7:1-4). Therefore, they should honor God with their body and honor their future spouse by avoiding sexual immorality.

Years ago, a woman was talking to me at the altar after church. I didn't think anything about it; people always talk to me after service. But when we got home, Sue said to me, "Honey that woman was hitting on you."

"What? You're kidding."

"Yeah," Sue said. "She was hitting on you. You're going to have to watch that with her."

I didn't believe Sue, at first, but I have since learned to listen to her. Sue has a sixth sense about such things. Sure enough, the very next service, that woman came down to the front again to talk to me—this time, half dressed. And she was definitely flirting with me. I couldn't believe it! I hadn't realized what was happening at first, but Sue did.

If people will hit on a preacher at church, they will most certainly hit on your spouse at work or groom your child at school. We must be sober and vigilant. The devil roams around in our culture looking for someone to devour (1 Peter 5:8). Notice again that 1 Corinthians 6:18 says, *"Flee sexual immorality."* Don't play with it or entertain it. Run! Don't let the world deceive and convince you that your kids are going to have sex and there's nothing you can do about it. Don't let culture teach your children that a condom will protect them from the consequences of sexual immorality. A condom cannot reverse God's Word. It does not protect from all venereal disease. It cannot stop all pregnancy. The only "safe sex" resides within the confines of marriage.

In sex, man and woman become one flesh. There is an exchange in their bodies and souls. It is a powerful experience, and it needs to be experienced within the safety of a lifetime commitment of marriage. Sex is like taking two pieces of paper and gluing them together. If you try to separate that paper, you will deface and damage both pieces. There is no such thing as "casual sex." The very phrase dismisses the beauty and bonding that occurs during sexual love.

Paul says that when you commit sexual sin, you sin against your own body, and the consequences of that sin come into the body as well. That's where we get gonorrhea and herpes, syphilis, chlamydia, and other STDs. Chlamydia and syphilis are at epidemic proportions in the United States. In 2022, HPV, a virus related to chlamydia, affected one in four sexually-active teenage girls. HPV was also responsible for 90 percent of all cervical cancers.[3]

During this same time, a television commercial was peddling a vaccine for HPV. But in typical smokescreen fashion, the ad only showed a loving mom and her young daughter visiting the doctor as a preventative measure. It left the audience with the impression that HPV just comes upon you, like a cold. Barely legible, in the fine print of the last screenshot, it said this virus is transmitted through sexual activity. It's just another example of how today's culture keeps trying to invent new ways to escape the consequences of sin, but can't.

In Romans 1:21, Paul explains the consequences of sexual perversion. Not only does it affect the body, but it also affects the mind. When people know there is a God and refuse to glorify Him or be thankful, their hearts become foolish and darkened. God gives them up to the lust of their hearts and they dishonor themselves and each other with their bodies (Romans 1:24, 26, 28). Lust leads to homosexuality and other perversions which Romans 1:27 says leads to, *"the penalty of their error."* Their immune system is compromised and they open themselves up to sexually transmitted diseases. Three times this passage mentions God *"giving them over"* to lust, and in their sin, receiving its just reward into their bodies. God doesn't do this to them. He doesn't strike them with these preventable diseases. They do it to themselves—not just in homosexuality, but in all sexual sin.

Every time you have sex with a person, you pick up their sexual history. Any viruses they have are passed on to you. The virus

---

[3] "Cancers Linked with HPV Each Year," *CDC.gov*, September 18, 2024; https://www.cdc.gov/cancer/hpv/cases.html; accessed March 26, 2025.

grows, and the more times you commit sexual sin, the higher your risk of contracting an STD becomes. That's why there were such harsh judgments on sexual perversion under the law. The consequences of that sin destroy the body and soul; and in time, will destroy a society. Just look at Sodom and Gomorrah (Genesis 19; Jude).

God would have saved Sodom and Gomorrah if He could have found ten righteous people within it. But Lot and his family were the only ones. God rescued them before invoking final judgment, but even His judgment was an act of mercy. That sin could have spread like cancer worldwide.

God cares about our bodies. He cares about our health and happiness. But He knows that wholeness is compromised with sexual immorality. God wants to spare us from the physical and emotional damage of premarital sex. He wants to sanctify us spirit, soul, and body (1 Thessalonians 5:23). But we have to believe and obey His Word.

20

THE MARRIAGE ALTAR

Have you not read that He who made them at the beginning "made them male and female," and said, "For this reason a man shall leave his father and mother and be joined to his wife, and the two shall become one flesh"?

—Matthew 19:4-5

Much of our teaching during the adolescent years is to prepare our children for marriage once they transition out of our care. That involves, not only an understanding of what marriage truly is and how to get to the marriage altar in a God-honoring way, but also a personal commitment to God's Word and a desire to keep growing and maturing in it. In this chapter, we look at the biblical principles of the marriage altar and how we can help our children successfully navigate to it.

Before we dive into these principles, keep in mind that no system is perfect. Neither is any human being—parent or child. We won't get all these things "right" all the time. However, we can rely on God's Word to offer wisdom and guidance for our success. In scripture, the principle of multiple witnesses was invoked in all high-risk decisions (Deuteronomy 17:6, 19:15; 1 Timothy 5:19). In biblical days, this usually involved independent, eyewitness testimony.

Today, we use other, more reliable, sources (things like fingerprinting, DNA matches, video recordings, etc.) to testify in a court of law. For *"Where there is no counsel, the people fall; but in the multitude of counselors there is safety"* (Proverbs 11:14). We can apply this principle to the high-risk decision of marriage as well.

Our first witness in choosing a spouse should be God—His Word and Spirit, which always agree. Does the person we are considering for marriage meet the requirements of scripture? Is the person a believer (2 Corinthians 6:14)? As an overseer in the home, is he temperate, sober, gentle, not covetous or greedy (1 Timothy 3:2-5)? As her husband's crown, is she virtuous, trustworthy, and industrious? Does she speak life (Proverbs 12:4; Proverbs 31)? Do both people understand and portray God's kind of love (1 Corinthians 13)?

Parents can be another witness. Ephesians 6:1-3 says, *"Children, obey your parents in the Lord, for this is right. Honor your father and mother which is the first commandment with promise: that it may be well with you and you may live long on the earth."* Of course, we have to be mindful to avoid both ditches connected to this verse as our children age. We shouldn't be the disengaged, passive parent who believes this decision belongs solely to our child. Remember, it can be hard for your child to discern motives and character when their emotions are involved.

But we must also not become the controlling parent who believes this decision belongs only to us. We don't have to live with whomever our child marries. We need to find the balance of these extremes so we can help protect our child and support them as they make wise decisions.

Spiritual authorities can be another witness in this process—from the teaching your child receives at church to the godly leaders who model what it is to have a successful marriage.

Spiritual leaders were a huge witness to Sue and me before we married. As was the premarital counseling they engaged in with us. It helped us see what a marriage should look like.

Ultimately your child, and his or her intended, will make the final decision about whether or not to marry. (They will be the ones living with the decision after all.) God has given us all a free will. And that doesn't just relate to our choice to believe and follow Him. It also pertains to whom we marry. Consider the story of Isaac and Rebekah in Genesis 24. Abraham sent a servant to his relative's house to look for a bride for his son. Abraham gave his servant a list of qualifications for the girl, but ultimately left the decision to Rebekah saying, *"If the woman is not willing to follow you, then you will be released from this oath…"* (Genesis 24:8).

BETROTHAL VERSUS DATING

In the institution of marriage, men leave the home and marry as adults, but women are given in marriage (Genesis 2:24; Mark 10:7; Psalm 78:63; Deuteronomy 22:16). To this day at weddings, fathers walk their daughters down the aisle and answer the question, "Who gives this woman in marriage?" Biblically, fathers are responsible for the preparation and giving of a bride.

(Deuteronomy 22:21 says, *"Then they shall bring out the young woman to the door of her father's house, and the men of her city shall stone her to death with stones, because she has done a disgraceful thing in Israel, to play the harlot in her father's house. So you shall put away the evil from among you."* This scripture deals with marital fraud—a girl proclaiming to be a virgin when she is not, and while we are thankful to not be under the curse of the law, is there not a message here for fathers? Fathers, guard your daughter's sexual purity and protect her from any who would abuse her.)

There's no such thing as "dating" in the Bible. Instead, couples were betrothed. Betrothal is the concept of a father giving his daughter in marriage by approving of her relationship with a man knowing the end goal will be marriage. Numbers 30 covers the role of fathers in a daughter's decision to marry or make other vows.

If a woman makes a vow to the Lord, and binds herself by some agreement while in her father's house in her youth, and her father hears her vow and the agreement by which she has bound herself, and her father holds his peace, then all her vows shall stand, and every agreement with which she has bound herself shall stand. But if her father overrules her on the day that he hears, then none of her vows nor her agreements by which she has bound herself shall stand; and the Lord will release her, because her father overruled her (Numbers 30:3-5).

God honors the authority of a father over his children. He respects that covering, which is why Satan wants to destroy the home and remove fathers from their God-given position. Satan wants to remove children from their protective covering to make them easier to devour.

I was directly involved in both of my daughters' decisions to marry. I gave my consent at their engagements and again at their weddings. This is traditionally why ministers ask if there is any who knows of a just cause why two people should not be married. The minister admonishes the congregation to "Speak now or forever hold your peace" because silence is approval.

Part of the betrothal process in scripture was the payment of a dowry. But unlike what became common practice in medieval Europe, the biblical dowry was the price a potential husband paid for his bride. (Somehow, in Europe, the custom switched, and women began bringing a dowry with them into marriage.)

In Genesis 34:11-12, Shechem asked for the hand of Dinah (a young woman he raped) begging her father, *"Let me find favor in your eyes, and whatever you say to me I will give. Ask me ever so much dowry and gift, and I will give according to what you say to me; but give me the young woman as a wife."* Shechem was willing to pay anything for Dinah, but Jacob still had to give his consent and blessing. In 1 Samuel 18:25-27, Saul required the foreskins of 100 Philistines as a dowry for his daughter Michal. And in Genesis 29:20, Jacob paid the largest dowry in history to marry Rachel—seven years of his life! Laban deceived Jacob by giving Leah the oldest daughter, so Jacob labored another seven years for Rachel.

Dowries proved three things. They proved a man's commitment to and willingness to sacrifice for a woman while showing his value of her. The higher the bride's price, the more he valued his intended, not in a property sort of way, but as a cherished relationship. The dowry also proved his ability to provide for his prospective wife. It forced him to plan and prepare for his future. The dowry was also a way to honor the girl's parents. It was a small token of appreciation for all they did to prepare her for marriage.

There is no mention of the dowry in New Testament instruction, but the principle of honor and respect that it communicated abounds; as does the man's need to provide for his wife and children (1 Timothy 5:8). Another qualification for marriage revealed in the New Testament is: *"Husbands, likewise, dwell with them with understanding, giving honor to the wife, as to the weaker vessel, and as being heirs together of the grace of life, that your prayers may not be hindered"* (1 Peter 3:7). There's that word *honor* again. But note, too, the word *understanding*. Husbands needs to come into the marriage relationship recognizing and celebrating the diversity between male and female. They need to understand and appreciate their wives and the unique role they will play in their life.

QUALIFICATIONS FOR MARRIAGE

I have touched on this briefly, but I wanted to spend more time on the qualifications that every believer should have for their intended spouse. First, and most importantly, a spouse must be a fellow believer (Genesis 24:3-4, 28:1-2; 1 Corinthians 9:5; 2 Corinthians 6:14-15; 1 Corinthians 7:39). Marrying outside the family of God is the equivalent of accepting a full-time call to the mission field. *"Do not be unequally yoked together with unbelievers. For what fellowship has righteousness with lawlessness? And what communion has light with darkness? And what accord has Christ with Belial? Or what part has a believer with an unbeliever?"* (2 Corinthians 6:14-15). When believers violate these instructions, they do so to their own demise.

Two seemingly opposite truths must also be reconciled in our minds before we can understand the roles attraction and agape love play in marriage. The first is that "opposites attract." The second is that "birds of a feather flock together." In marriage, it is very common for men and women to have opposite personality types. I believe this is by design. It helps us complement one another and creates a synergy that makes us better together than apart (1 Corinthians 12:7).

When, as diverse people, we come together in unity, life becomes infinitely more fruitful. A good example of this is reproduction. Men and women's bodies are different. But when united in diversity (sexual intimacy) they bear much fruit. They make babies. We can't bear fruit in sameness. Fruit requires diversity working together in unity.

Though this diversity is a good thing, there must still be common ground for a marriage to work. *Birds of a feather flock together.* Why? Because the birds are all going the same way! In marriage, we need to go the same way as well. We need to follow after the Spirit and agree over the basic foundations of life:

- God exists as He is revealed in scripture.
- Jesus is both Lord and personal Savior.
- God's Word is the final authority.
- Absolute truth exists in Christ.
- Marriage is a covenant, not a contract. (It lasts until death not until someone burns the bacon. We partner together understanding that there will be problems, but also committed to working those problems out together.)

Marriage is a picture of Christ and the Church (Ephesians 5:32). As believers, we need to marry believers as a witness of this truth. Marriage is not just a physical union. It is spiritual. It is a covenant agreement; two becoming one (Amos 3:3; Mark 10:8). Like a good father, God does not give us these principles and requirements to constrain or harm us. He gives them for our protection. We should teach them to our children for the same reason.

21

A BIBLICAL VIEW ON SEX

Marriage is honorable among all, and the bed undefiled; but fornicators and adulterers God will judge.

—*Hebrews 13:4*

We've briefly talked about the beauty of sexual love within marriage and God's blessings in that contrasted with the danger of sex outside marriage. But nowhere in scripture can I think of a verse that so succinctly describes this dichotomy than Hebrews 13:4. *"Marriage is honorable among all, and the bed undefiled; but fornicators and adulterers God will judge."* This verse showcases God's blessing on sex within the bonds of marriage and the judgment that arises when sex is taken outside those bounds.

Why do we have to cover this topic? You may be asking. *We figured it out, surely our children can, too.* Self-discovery may have worked during the generation when people just got married and had fun figuring it out, but today is not that day. Times are not as innocent as they once were. The lions of culture have encircled our children and are ready to pounce—from preschool onward. And while God does not give us a spirit of fear, we need to remain sober and vigilant to protect them from these predators (1 Peter 5:8-9). We need discernment and wisdom as we walk by faith knowing that God's protection rests on our children—but also accepting our responsibility to teach them His ways and prepare them for what they will encounter outside our home. Our children are in the lion's den. But God has given us principles and specific boundaries to equip them for success.

In the book of Revelation, the angel speaking with John says that in the end time, people will become drunk on sexual perversion and idolatry (Revelation 17:1-2). When not kept in check (which they have not been), these things become *"a dwelling place of demons"* (Revelation 18:2). Libraries and other government entities are peddling sex to children in the form of drag queen story times and free-access pornography. They are grooming children for sex trafficking and sexual perversion to destroy their God-given destinies. These places have become like Babylon, a dwelling place for demons and foul spirits. Revelation 18:3 reads, *"For all the nations have drunk of the wine of the wrath of her fornication, the kings of the earth have committed fornication with her, and the merchants of the earth have become rich through the abundance of her luxury."* Does that not sound like our world system? Every year, billions of dollars are made off child porn, illicit sex, and sex trafficking. It has become a drug; the world is intoxicated with fornication and unable to think rationally.

Satan has twisted the original purpose of sex and is using it to bring down kings, presidents, business leaders, and ministers. There is no greater challenge as a parent than to raise children in sexual purity. One day a week at church will not prepare them for Babylon's wine. We must be engaged. And even after our children are married, we must remain vigilant in prayer for ourselves and our families. Sexual perversion does not end with marriage. Even there we have to guard against adultery, pornography, incest, and pedophilia. Pedophilia is at an all-time high in our country. This sexual tolerance has released predators to prey upon our children—both in person and online. We must oversee our children's computers, phones, and social media interactions. Nothing should be personal or hidden from your eyes. (After four decades of marriage, Sue still has every right to view my text messages, emails, and other social media communication.)

But sex is not all bad and ugly. When confined to its proper boundaries, sex is a gift from God. And we need to teach our children that truth as well. *"Therefore, shall a man leave his father and his mother, and shall cleave unto his wife, and they shall be one flesh. And they were both naked, the man and his wife, and were not ashamed"* (Genesis 2:24-25). Notice that this verse mentions man and wife, father and mother. That is God's good plan for humankind—the covenant partnership of marriage and enjoying our sexuality together as husband and wife. Jesus even quoted this passage of scripture thousands of years later as He taught on marriage in Mark 10:1-9.

Marriage was created by God between the two genders, male and female. Sex, too, was created by Him. God created sex before sin came into the world. It was His gift to man, and in their sinless state, the man and woman were naked and unashamed. The devil didn't create sex. Rather he corrupted a precious and beautiful gift from God.

The Hebrew word translated as *cleave* in Genesis 2 literally means to pursue, be glued together, and united. It is a picture of sexual love. Sex is a gift from God, and like any gift, it comes with an owner's manual—God's Word, the Bible. The Song of Solomon describes the pleasures of sexual love between a husband and wife. It is racy and graphic. But it is also holy and pure. How? Because the pleasures it describes take place within the covenant of marriage, exactly as God intended. And that should be the goal of every Christian parent—both within their marriage and for their children—purity. It takes work. It requires diligence, but it is worth it.

There are basically three viewpoints on sex and human sexuality: the world's viewpoint, the religious viewpoint, and God's viewpoint. Let's look at each:

1. World's Viewpoint

Sex is a god of this world. People live, dream, and work for sex. They are intoxicated with the wine of fornication. They want sex without boundaries, consequences, or moral judgment. This perversion is a form of idolatry, and it keeps many from salvation. Sexual addiction locks people into death, yet God's Word is clear. Judgment will come to all who practice such behavior—even in the church. Do not ignore scripture's warning for yourself and your children's sake. (Read Ephesians 4–5; 1 Corinthians 6:9-11, 18; Colossians 3:5; Hebrews 13:4; Romans 6:12; 2 Corinthians 12:21).

2. Religious Viewpoint

The religious view on sex can be just as unhealthy. Religion views sex as impure, even in marriage. They think sex is for procreation only, and many women are taught they must endure it to have children. This view is entirely unbiblical. Proverbs 5:18-20 says,

> ...rejoice with the wife of your youth. As a loving deer and a graceful doe, let her breasts satisfy you at all times; and always be enraptured with her love. For why should you, my son,

be enraptured by an immoral woman, and be embraced in the arms of a seductress?

Song of Solomon also showcases the romance, for both a husband and wife, of love. Wives are supposed to experience pleasure in sexual love (Genesis 18:12). Sex is important for a healthy marriage, and it is a healthy part of a marriage. It's not hard to have sex without marriage, but it is hard to have a marriage without sex. Couples who are not having sex are not happily married. They are not following scripture's mandate to become one flesh. Sex offers spouses a physical, emotional, and spiritual bond of intimacy that cannot be replicated in other ways. If you find somebody with a healthy, happy marriage, they're having good sex and they're having sex often. And I will leave it at that.

3. God's Viewpoint

God has plenty to say about our sexuality. He has not left it a mystery or told us to just figure it out. Yet I am amazed how little is said about sex at church. Hebrews 13:4 says,

Marriage is honorable among all, and the bed undefiled; but fornicators and adulterers God will judge.

God's perspective covers both sides of sex. In marriage, it is honorable among all, whether you are saved or lost. Marriage and sexuality in marriage is a gift from God, for everyone, not just the Church. That's why I defend the institution of marriage. It was given to all. Sexual love is one of the many things that separate us from animals. Animals mate; we make love. When two lost people get married, God sanctifies their sexuality. He gives them a taste of heaven on earth. But fornicators and adulterers, those practicing sex outside of marriage, God will judge. There is no such thing as casual sex; neither is there sex without moral judgment. That's why your children need to learn to control their sexuality before they get married. They can't have sex with coworkers, children, family members, neighbors, animals, or anything else outside their marriage covenant. Sexual purity—both before and after marriage—is God's will. The Passion Translation of Hebrews 13:4 says,

> *Honor the sanctity of marriage and keep your vows of purity to one another, for God will judge sexual immorality in any form, whether single or married.*

THE ARK OF THE COVENANT

When the Philistines stole the Ark of the Covenant, they thought they had defeated God. They parked the Ark before their false god, Dagon. The next morning their idol had fallen over. They picked it up, but the next day its arms and head fell off. Curses began coming upon the Philistines. Rats and tumors infected their land and people, so the people called for the Ark to be sent back to where it came from. It had brought nothing but trouble upon them (1 Samuel 5).

When David became king, he left with 30,000 men to recover the Ark. But he didn't follow God's pattern in doing so. He made a new cart and danced before the Ark as oxen pulled it toward Jerusalem. The ox stumbled and Uzzah, who was not a Levite, reached out to keep the Ark from falling. He touched the Ark and died. David freaked out. He became angry with the Lord and afraid of Him (2 Samuel 6:8-9).

David parked the Ark at Obed Edom's house until he could figure out what to do. For three months, this man and his household experienced the blessing of God. His marriage was blessed; his kids were blessed. All his flocks and herds were blessed. Obed Edom began to multiply, and when David heard about it, he returned to Obed Edom's house to collect the Ark. This time as God ordained, with priests carrying it back to Jerusalem. No one died. And there was great joy in the city. The difference? David related to the Ark properly (2 Samuel 6; 1 Chronicles 15).

Think about this for a minute. The Philistines didn't relate properly to the Ark and they were cursed. Uzzah did not relate properly to it and died. Obed Edom did relate properly to the Ark, and everything he touched was blessed. Sex works the same way. How you relate to it determines whether or not it will be a blessing to you.

I always told my children that sex was good. A gift from God. Sex is pure and holy within its proper boundaries. But if you relate to sex improperly, it can destroy you. It can destroy your family. I taught 1 Thessalonians 4:1-5 (NLT):

> *Finally, dear brothers and sisters, we urge you in the name of the Lord Jesus to live in a way that pleases God, as we have taught you. You live this way already, and we encourage you to do so even more. For you remember what we taught you by the authority of the Lord Jesus. God's will is for you to be holy, so stay away from all sexual sin. Then each of you will control his own body and live in holiness and honor—not in lustful passion like the pagans who do not know God and his ways.*

This command came by the authority of Jesus. It was not just a human opinion. Sexual purity and boundaries are about holiness, for our bodies belong to God. First Thessalonians 4:6-8 (NLT) as well:

Never harm or cheat a fellow believer in this matter by violating his wife, for the Lord avenges all such sins, as we have solemnly warned you before. God has called us to live holy lives, not impure lives. Therefore, anyone who refuses to live by these rules is not disobeying human teaching but is rejecting God, who gives his Holy Spirit to you.

When a young person commits sexual sin, they dishonor their parents. They dishonor God. They dishonor their own body and that of their future mate. Sexual purity is about honoring God and saving ourselves for marriage—not so we can be self-righteous prudes, but so we can please the Lord and experience the blessing of His gift of sex.

God is working on a future spouse for your child. Don't you want that mate to be pure and holy? Don't you want them to be free from venereal diseases? Then your child needs to prepare themselves for his or her mate as well. It's a command of the Lord, not my opinion. We all need to know how to honor our God-given bodies. If a young person cannot control their emotions before they get married, what makes us think after marriage they will be able to? They won't. They'll be tempted with affairs, pornography, workplace flirtations, and snares.

Unfortunately, when most young people fail in this area, they give up. "I'm not a virgin anymore. Why try to live holy?" Don't let this happen to your child. Teach them that mistakes don't define us. God is merciful and forgiving. All we have to do is repent. Push the restart button, and don't allow failure to become a permanent address (Proverbs 24:16). And if you have failed in your sexuality as a parent, do not disqualify yourself or allow guilt and condemnation to keep you from teaching your children. Receive forgiveness and serve your children well.

22

PREPARING FOR MARRIAGE

By wisdom a house is built and by understanding it is established; through knowledge its rooms are filled with every precious and beautiful treasure.

—Proverbs 24:3-4 Berean Standard Bible

In my book *Better Together*, I teach the seven areas of marital breakdown: 1) security and trust; 2) communication; 3) forgiveness and repentance; 4) finances and values; 5) roles and responsibilities; 6) raising children; and 7) sex and romance. I discovered each of these hurdles (and the principles that help us work through them) through decades of premarital counseling. I firmly believe no one should enter marriage unprepared. However, I also realize that we are never fully prepared for any new venture; some things can only be learned on the battlefield of life. So how do we help prepare our children for marriage?

Part of our preparation process should be the development of a "grow together" mindset. Before Sue and I married, we knew we would face problems. A big part of our success has been our commitment to face those problems together. The process of two people becoming one always causes friction. But if we lay solid foundations before marriage, we can overcome any challenge that arises with resolve and wisdom, as long as we remain in unity.

In this chapter, I highlight six of the areas of marital breakdown and the biblical principles that will prepare our children to overcome them in their own marriages. (I won't be covering "raising children" in this chapter since this entire book has been about that subject.) I believe preparing for these areas is an important step our children should take before getting married. Keep in mind, however, that though these areas are common to us all, we view them differently as male and female.

Still the one-flesh principle God gave in marriage requires that we become united in our diversity. What do I mean by that? We need to acknowledge and appreciate the differences we bring into marriage and leverage them for our good and His glory. We need to come into agreement, prior to marriage, about the fundamental truths of these areas. I greatly respect the differences between Sue and I and firmly believe that I am a better person because of them. The diversity in our personalities and gifts has strengthened us both and allowed us to accomplish more for God's kingdom. But if we had not been able to find agreement in these things, our marriage would have suffered.

SECURITY AND TRUST

Security and trust are built in relationships of shared commitment and mutual understanding. When we enter marriage, we understand that divorce is no option; that foundation of commitment creates safety and sets our marriage up to last.

We must teach our children that marriage is a covenant not a contract (Malachi 2:14). We should never enter marriage lightly or think we can exit out of it easily. Whatever problems we face, we have to know both parties will face them head-on. No one will run. Without this principle of commitment in marriage, couples will not overcome the struggles of making one flesh out of two. They will always dream of and look for an easier way out. But there is no plan B in marriage (Hebrews 11:15).

Communication

Human beings were created with the ability and need for communication. Yet many of us fail in this skill. As parents, part of our job is to prepare our children for success in life and marriage by teaching them effective communication strategies. Every interaction they have with siblings, teachers, friends, bosses, pastors, and even us is a hands-on apprenticeship in communication. To be effective in this area, our children need to learn how to talk (it's harder than you think), listen, give and receive feedback, and in all things be honest yet kind. I devoted an entire chapter to this skill earlier in the book, so I'll just briefly mention them here:

Talk

You'd be surprised how difficult it is to learn to talk to others. Talking is not grunting, murmuring, complaining, shouting, or verbally assaulting others. It is the civil verbalization of one's thoughts and ideas. It involves tone, attitude, and eye contact. It requires respect and vulnerability. And it takes practice to learn to talk *to* others instead of *at* them.

Listen

Listening is skilled art. It involves choice—as Jesus says in Mark 4:23—and a willingness to understand. We have to have *"an ear to hear."* James 1:19 (NIV) says, *"My dear brothers and sisters, take note of this: Everyone should be quick to listen, slow to speak and slow to become angry."* Listening involves discernment. It is being fully present and engaged in a conversation. It asks questions as a means to understanding. "What do you mean by this?" "Can you explain that again?" "Tell me more." Listening has become a lost art in our culture. For some reason, culture has bought into the lie that you have to agree to understand. But that is not true.

FEEDBACK

Feedback is vital to communication. Feedback clarifies what was said, uncovers what was heard, and seeks to discover meaning. It reveals misunderstandings and wrong applications in our attempts at communication. Without feedback loops, we can't know if our communication has been effective.

HONESTY

Honesty can be the most challenging aspect of communication for a host of reasons. People fear being misunderstood or judged. They don't want to offend or hurt anyone's feelings, so they tend to withhold the truth. Others, in the name of truth, are brutal and unkind in their communication. Neither practice is fruitful. We have to learn to speak the truth in love, so we don't create more problems than we solve. Phrases like, "When you say that you make me feel…" and "Give me a moment. I'm trying to respond to your words, not your tone" can help your children find the balance between honesty and kindness. We need to be honest with our thoughts, feelings, and opinions while also giving others the benefit of the doubt, not assigning motivation or blame to their words. And when we are on the giving end of communication, we need to be careful not to purposefully deceive or lie by default (Colossians 3:9). One tries to cover up fault or protect and promote self. The other withholds truth to prevent misunderstandings. Both are wrong, and part of the old self we are called to take off.

Forgiveness and Repentance

Repentance and forgiveness are the foundation of pure Christianity. It's how we are saved but also how we are to represent Christ to others. Repentance is the key to a happy, fulfilled life. Learning to own our mistakes and apologize as needed is the only way to build healthy relationships. But the other side of that skill is forgiveness. We need to learn to forgive others—whether or not they ask. Forgiveness releases another of debt. It allows us to move on without the toxicity of anger and bitterness. This is doubly important in marriage. Marriage is the only relationship where our flesh is exposed 24 hours a day, seven days a week. If our children learn early in life to repent and forgive, they will prosper in their marriages.

Finances and Value

Everyone must learn to live within their means, manage debt, make goals, and use a budget. But finances can put an undo strain on marriage, namely because of our differences in perceived value. Men and women view finances and debt differently. While we don't have to feel the same way about what is a good use of our extra money, as husbands and wives we need to honor and support one another as an expression of God's love. We need to develop a shared understanding of how we will steward finances (tithing, savings, investments, expenses, hobbies, etc.) and meet our financial goals. Children should be prepared for these discussions by learning to handle finances and overcome the temptation of covetousness (1 Timothy 6:9).

Roles and Responsibilities

Another area of marital breakdown happens when couples do not know their roles and responsibilities in marriage. The primary role of a husband is to love his wife. And the primary role of a wife is to respect her husband (Ephesians 5:33). If we do these things well, we will meet one another's needs—physical and emotional. Choosing who plans and cooks meals or who manages the checkbook is an act of grace. Who enjoys those activities? Who is better at them? If we are following the biblical mandate to love and respect, we have the freedom to choose how we practically structure our homes. But we never have the freedom to condemn someone else for structuring theirs differently.

As parents we need to teach our children that men and women have different emotional needs. Wives need love—emotional, romantic, and affectionate love. Love is how they bond. Husbands need respect. If we want to bond more with our spouses, we need to recognize their need for love or respect. Unloving husbands and disrespectful wives do not do well in marriage. We need to teach our boys to love their families unselfishly, and we need to teach our girls how to be respectful, especially in disagreements. Children learn these things best when they see them modeled by their parents. Children need to see Dad loving on Mom. They need to see him pursuing and dating her. Children also need to see Mom respecting Dad's authority and oversight of the home.

Men need to lead in love. Wives need to follow in respectful submission (Ephesians 5:21-33).

SEX AND ROMANCE

Men and women also have different needs as it pertains to sex and romance. While there are exceptions to every rule, men typically need sexual love and wives typically crave romantic love. God addressed this the moment He created marriage in Genesis 2:24-25: *"Therefore a man shall leave his father and his mother and shall **cleave** unto his wife, and they shall be one flesh. And they were both naked, the man and his wife, and were not ashamed."* Cleave is a Hebrew word that means both "to catch by pursuit" (romance) and "to cling or be glued to" (sex). In marriage, both the man and woman are to enjoy their physical relationship without guilt or shame. Paul talks about this issue as well:

> Let the husband render to his wife the affection due her, and likewise also the wife to her husband. The wife does not have authority over her own body, but the husband does. And likewise the husband does not have authority over his own body, but the wife does. Do not deprive one another except with consent for a time, that you may give yourselves to fasting and prayer; and come together again so that Satan does not tempt you because of your lack of self-control (1 Corinthians 7:3-5).

Sex is part of marriage and part of serving one another in love. Girls need to be taught that a man's sexual drive may be stronger than hers. He will want to have sex, and she needs to make herself available for that so he doesn't fall into temptation. Boys need to be taught that a woman needs romance. A ring does not cure that need. Women need their husbands to pursue and date them for a lifetime. She will respond to kindness, touch, and affection, and he needs to be there to meet that need.

Communication is a vital piece of the puzzle in this area. So, if a person cannot communicate those needs to their intended, they need to wait to marry. While sex exists outside love and marriage, marriage cannot survive without love and sex. Understanding these principles can help prepare your children for marriage, highlighting the person who will make a compatible mate or revealing those whom they should not marry—either of which is a blessing.

Conclusion

While I have previously stated that there are no perfect children or parents, if you have made it this far—you are awesome! These teachings cover 20 years of child-rearing and loving oversight. I pray this book becomes a resource to revisit often throughout your and your child's journey in life. Your care and concern to even seek wisdom in this area of ministry for your children is a testament of your love for God and your children.

Parenting can be a daunting undertaking as well as a joy unspeakable lasting a lifetime. The labor of love and work of faith along with patience and hope has brought generational blessings to my wife and me. Seeing evident fruit in both our children and grandchildren is pure joy and pleasure. During times of difficulty and discouragement, remember to "keep the faith" and ask the Lord for strength and endurance. I promise you there is light at the end of the tunnel—and it's not another train headed your way.

Children can have their moments or seasons of acting up or out. It will pass—and if you stay consistent, unwavering, immovable in the Lord, I guarantee your labor in the Lord will not be in vain. The following is a prayer you can pray over yourself in this role of raising godly warriors:

Father, thank You for helping me to be a wise parent for my child. Strengthen me in this fight of faith. Help me to be consistent in discipline with love and patience while listening to the leading of Your voice in each season of life. May my children rise to be godly warriors in a dark world, shining the light of the goodness of God. AMEN!

About Duane Sheriff

Duane Sheriff has more than four decades of ministry experience and is known for his humor and ability to present the Gospel with clarity and simplicity. He is passionate about helping people discover their identity and grow in Christ through his unique biblical insight.

Duane is an author, international apostolic teacher, conference speaker, adjunct instructor at Charis Bible College, and the host of his daily broadcast Grace & Truth. He founded Victory Life Church in Durant, Oklahoma, where he served as senior pastor for more than 30 years and is now the lead communicator and an elder.

Duane and his wife, Sue, have been married for more than 40 years and have four children. He enjoys hunting and spending time with his grandchildren.

In the Right Hands, This Book Will Change Lives!

Most of the people who need this message will not be looking for this book. To change their lives, you need to **put a copy of this book in their hands.**

Our ministry is constantly seeking methods to find the people who need this anointed message to change their lives. **Will you help us reach these people?**

Extend this ministry by sowing three, five, ten, or *even more* books today and change people's lives for the better! Your generosity will be part of catalyzing the Great Awakening that many have been prophesying and praying for.

YOUR HOUSE OF
FAITH

Sign up for a **FREE** subscription to the Harrison House digital magazine and get excellent content delivered directly to your inbox!

harrisonhouse.com/signup

Sign up for Messages that Equip You to Walk in the Abundant Life

- Receive biblically sound and Spirit-filled encouragement to focus on and maintain your faith
- Grow in faith through biblical teachings, prayers, and other spiritual insights
- Connect with a community of believers who share your values and beliefs

Experience Fresh Teachings and Inspiration to Build Your Faith

- Deepen your understanding of God's purpose for your life
- Stay connected and inspired on your faith journey
- Learn how to grow spiritually in your walk with God

Check out
our **Harrison House**
bestsellers page at
harrisonhouse.com/bestsellers
for fresh,
faith-building messages
that will equip you
to walk in the
abundant life.